London's
Lea Valley

First published in 2019 by Redshank Books

ISBN 978-1-912969-07-4

Cover and Design by Helen Taylor and Carnegie Book Production

Printed in the UK by Severn

Redshank Books
Brunel House
Volunteer Way
Faringdon
Oxfordshire
SN7 7YR

Tel: +44 (0)845 873 3837

www.libripublishing.co.uk

London's Lea Valley

Home of Britain's Growing Food and Drink Industry and a Little Bit More!

Jim Lewis

Foreword by Dr Joy Kettyle

As the residing Principal of Waltham Forest College, it is both an honour and a pleasure to have been invited to write this foreword. Waltham Forest College, founded in 1938, has been a centre for culinary arts in the heart of the Waltham Forest community. It has been the starting point for many budding chefs who have gone on to achieve great accomplishments in their subsequent careers.

Alumni Rani King MBE, FRSA is one such student who was inspired by her time at Waltham Forest College's Catering School, studying Hotels and Catering in 1977. Rani went on to run a number of restaurants, write and co-author books on South East Asian Cooking and appear on British television as a celebrity chef on numerous occasions. She remains a friend of the College to this day.

Secondly, I want to recognise the many great successes of Alyn Williams, whose culinary career was inspired by his time also at Waltham Forest College's Catering School, which included a placement at Claridge's Hotel. His career progressed through various Michelin Starred kitchens before he returned to Claridge's in 2001 to work for Gordon Ramsay. He states…

> "As a youngster I was a bit of a tearaway and as I developed as a chef I found that a military-style organisation in the kitchen was what I personally needed, thriving on the pressure and discipline."

> *Aylin Williams, Michelin Chef*

Through his restaurant, Alyn Williams at the Westbury, he now mentors aspiring chefs enrolled on the catering course at Waltham Forest College who are also following in his footsteps.

One of Alyn's mentees, Aneta Styrkacz is the third success story I want to refer to. Aneta started her career in catering when she joined us on the Catering Level 1 course in 2015, eventually progressing to Level 2.

As part of her course she completed 4 weeks of work experience with Alyn Williams. After completing her Level 2 course, Aneta went on to work for Alyn full-time. Within a year she was promoted to Commis Chef and later to Demi Chef De Partie, training across different sections in the kitchen. She has noted of how the College played an instrumental part in kick starting her career in catering and she now aspires to run her own restaurant in London.

Waltham Forest College has a long history of inspiring learners to create their futures. The College strives in continuing to build and maintain relationships within the Catering Industry. These relationships, combined with recent investments in state-of-the-art kitchens and facilities, means Waltham Forest College will continue to support, train and develop great chefs like Aneta, who can move into meaningful employment and thrive in the industry.

The College also delivers apprenticeships and training in butchery. Apprentices can train on campus, learning their trade from expert butchers in a fully equipped and air-conditioned butchery room.

Over the last 20 years Waltham Forest College has trained over 200 butchers with successful apprentices going on to work in independent butcher shops, retail chains and catering.

I am very proud that in 2019 the College joined the local community in celebrating Waltham Forest becoming the first London Borough of Culture. And so this book couldn't have been published at a better time, as food (and by extension the Catering Industry) is a huge driving force for culture and it is my belief that Waltham Forest College will continue to support the Catering Industry in the Lea Valley region going into the future.

Dr Joy Kettyle
Principal and CEO
Waltham Forest College

Foreword by Terry Farrell

Jim Lewis is an extraordinary man. He is a traveller in that long tradition of indefatigable British explorers, journeying intellectually into unknown yet fascinating territory. Out of the glorious and chaotic metropolis that is London, Jim has discovered in his travels and revealed through his writing one of the great wonders of London – the extraordinary history of the Lea Valley.

The Lea Valley is the place where Jim spent his working life. The places he worked, and the characters he encountered there, drew him into the fascinating history of the place and inspired him to reveal the full story. I first encountered Jim through my own research into the Lea Valley, as part of my work in place making and characterisation of the Thames Gateway. Little did I know I could spend a lifetime struggling to learn only a fraction of what Jim has discovered.

Jim is a relentless advocate for this extraordinary place. For many years, he has been campaigning to seek recognition for the significance of the Lea Valley, as part of the rich history of London. For this small part of London changed the world – a crucible of scientific discovery and industrial firsts. His earlier books tell the unique story of the region, its scientists, engineers and entrepreneurs. But most significantly, Jim has revealed how the Lea Valley was the birthplace of the post-industrial revolution – the electronic technological revolution – which arguably began in the Lea Valley with the invention of the diode valve by Professor Ambrose Fleming. This small but inspired device allowed, for the first time, the control of a stream of electrons by electronic means, paving the way for modern electronic communication around the world and across the vast expanse of space.

Given the focus on the Lea Valley with the creation of the Queen Elizabeth Olympic Park, Jim is unique in the way he has recognised the significance of the place. In his last book, *The Factory that Became a Village, The History of the Royal Small Arms Factory at Enfield Lock* Jim traced the story of the RSAF site and took us on a fascinating two hundred-year trek through the challenges and politics of weapon development that ended in a good news story for a redundant and unloved historical building. Now, in this new publication he introduces us to another little-known Lea Valley story of a growing regional food and drinks industry. Therefore, I urge you to journey with him through a past which is shaping the future. It is people like Dr Jim Lewis who keep alive the magic of the place for present and future generations.

Sir Terry Farrell

ABOUT THE AUTHOR

Dr Jim Lewis has spent most of his career in the consumer electronics industry, apart from a three-year spell in the Royal Air Force servicing airborne and ground wireless communications equipment. When working in the Lea Valley for Thorn EMI Ferguson he represented the company abroad on several occasions and was involved in the exchange of manufacturing technology. Currently he is a Consultant to Terry Farrell & Partners on the historical development of London's Lea Valley. He is also a volunteer with Social Services teaching students who have learning difficulties. A freelance writer (with fourteen published books), researcher and broadcaster for his specialist subject – London's Lea Valley – he also has a genuine passion for encouraging partnership projects within the local community, which, in the long term, are planned to help stimulate social and economic regeneration.

In 2012 Dr Lewis was appointed Contributory International Professor by the Clark H. Byrum School of Business, Marian University, Indianapolis, for his work with students on The Modern British Service Economy.

Dr Lewis is married with four grown-up children and lives in Lincolnshire.

Jim Lewis with Robert Elms, presenter at BBC Radio London, after a live studio broadcast

INTRODUCTION

The post-war years saw a massive decline in the Lea Valley's industrial base. This was particularly marked by the collapse in furniture, electronics and electrical manufacturing that had been affected by cheap imports from countries abroad who had developed and streamlined their industries during the war years. Also affecting the collapse was a reluctance by some British manufacturers to invest and update their businesses in the light of the increasing overseas competition; these businesses seemed to take the attitude that the world at large owned them a living. This had been based on Britain's pre-war industrial market dominance and performance which was a carryover from the great Victorian period.

However, in recent years, in spite of all of these setbacks, the Lea Valley has seen a marked increase in the manufacture, development and distribution of food and drink products within the region. This upsurge has, in a way, complemented the work of earlier food and drink producers, several of whom have increased their product range and are now not only supplying and sustaining the British consumer markets, but also a number of markets overseas.

In this book we will not only uncover the Lea Valley's emerging food and drink industry, but we shall also highlight the history of those regional establishments that provided sustenance for earlier generations. Also, the opportunity will be taken to remind ourselves of those regional businesses which are still evolving and providing us with food and drink today. To do this the book will be split into three parts. The first section will cover those early industries and establishments, many of which have now gone without trace, the second will cover those early industries and establishments that have survived and the third will be about the new, and the relatively new kids on the block. To achieve these goals, we shall revisit and update some of the stories that I have previously written, bringing them all together in one book.

However, it will not be possible to cover every food retailer, manufacturer, wholesaler and microbrewery within the Lea Valley region in this publication as several of these new operations are at the planning stages as I write. Nevertheless, it is hoped that those establishments mentioned in this book will give the reader a "flavour" of how the valley's food and drink industries are evolving and changing. In fact, it would seem that before this book has reached the printer, another microbrewery has popped up or a new food wholesaler, manufacturer and distributor has emerged.

ACKNOWLEDGEMENTS

The author wishes to thank the following organisations, companies, societies and individuals for their encouragement, support and advice and for supplying many of the illustrations within this book:

Adrian Williams, Director, Cattlegate Farm, Cattlegate Road, Enfield EN2 8AU

Beverley Charters, The House Mill, Three Mill Lane, Bromley-by-Bow, Newham

Beavertown Brewery, PR Department, Mill Mead Road, Tottenham, London

Bruce Castle Museum, Bruce Grove Road, Tottenham, London

Camden Town Brewery, PR Department, Kentish Town, London

Caroline & John Jones, owners of Guy & Wright Ltd, Green Tye, Hertfordshire

Edmonton Hundred Historical Society, Enfield, Middlesex

Enfield Archaeological Society, Enfield, Middlesex

John Clark, Enfield Local History Unit, Thomas Hardy House, London Road, Enfield, Middlesex

Epping Forest Museum, Sun Street, Waltham Abbey, Essex

David Wright, Managing Director, G. R. Wright & Sons Ltd Ponders End Mills, Enfield, Middlesex EN3 4TG

Dawn Bennett, Head of Catering & Hospitality and Tom Barden, Graphic Designer and Marketing Officer, Waltham Forest College, Forest Road, Walthamstow, London E17

Greggs Bakery Ltd, Bakery and Distribution Centre, Millmarsh Lane, Enfield

Jimmy and Vince Russo, owners of Valley Grown Salads, Nazelow Nursery, Sedge Green Road, Roydon, Essex CM19 5JS

Julian Davis, Marketing Manager, Wanis International Foods, Unit One, Golden Business Park, Orient Way, Leyton, London E10 7FE

Lance Forman, MD of H. Forman & Son, Stour Road, Fish Island, London E3 2NT

Lee Styles, Secretary, Lea Valley Growers' Association, Cheshunt, Hertfordshire

Lee Valley Regional Park Authority, Myddelton House, Enfield, Middlesex

London Borough of Enfield, Civic Centre, Enfield, Middlesex

London Borough of Haringey, Civic Centre, Haringey, London

London Borough of Newham, Town Hall Annex, Barking Road, East Ham, London

London Borough of Waltham Forest, Town Hall, Forest Road, Walthamstow, London

Markfield Beam Engine & Museum, Markfield Park, Tottenham, London

Museum of London, London Wall, London

Philip Paul, Joint Managing Director, Snowbird Foods, Ponders End, Enfield

RCHME Cambridge, (National Monuments Record), Brooklands Avenue, Cambridge

Sainsbury's Press Office, Sainsbury's Stores Support Centre, 33 Holborn, London EC1N 2HT

Tazaki Foods, 12 Innova Way, Innova Park, Enfield EN3 7FL

Terry Larkin, General Sales Manager, JJ Food Services, Solar Way, Innova Park, Enfield EN3 7XY

Tesco Press Office, Tesco House, Shire Park, Kestrel Way, Welwyn Garden City, Hertfordshire AL7 1GA

Thames Water, Gainsborough House, Manor Farm Road, Reading, Berkshire

The Greater London Record Office, Northampton Road, London

The Hackney Society, Eleanor Road, Hackney, London

The House of Lords Record Office, Westminster, London

The National Archive, Kew, Richmond, Surrey

Tower Hamlets Local History Library, Bancroft Road, Tower Hamlets, London

Vasilis Nicouzos, Manager, Warburtons Bakeries Ltd, Delta Park, 112 Millmarsh Lane, Enfield

While many individuals have freely given their knowledge, some unknowingly, which has contributed greatly to the production of this series of books, I have, on a number of occasions paid special tribute to certain people in the footnotes of various chapters.

I could not let the occasion pass without recording my sincere thanks to my wife Jenny for her superb editorial skills and outstanding patience. The author freely admits that this voluntary sacrifice on Jenny's part has comprehensively tested the cement that holds our wonderful marriage together.

CONTENTS

PART ONE

(HISTORICAL FOOD AND DRINK CONNECTIONS THAT HAVE GONE)

THE BOW BREWERY

Now buried below a 1930s block of London County Council (LCC) flats, just south of the Bow flyover, is the footprint of a forgotten brewery. This site is the origin of a little-known story of a Lea Valley brewer, George Hodgson, and it is particularly sad when visiting a friendly public house and having a pint of a favourite ale pulled only to learn that nobody has heard of him and, to make matters worse, the spotty youth behind the bar pulling the pint cannot explain what the initials on the cellar pump handle stand for!

When the East India Company's docks were built at Blackwall on the Thames, Hodgson's Bow Brewery was already situated less than a mile north on the banks of the River Lea close to Bow Bridge. Hodgson's father had formed the brewing business in October 1752 and George had taken over from him in March 1754. Since the late 17th century beer had been exported from Britain to India and by the early 19th century the quantity shipped was recorded as rising to 9,000 barrels a year, a thirteen-fold increase on that shipped previously. Hodgson's brewery had been responsible for most of these increases in shipments and this was probably due to an improved formula that he had devised for his export beer.

Until the introduction of refrigeration plant during the mid-19th century the bulk brewing of beer in hot climates was an impossible task. The early beers that had been exported to India and elsewhere tended to be those commonly drunk in Britain over the previous hundred or so years and were of the dark heavy porter variety. This type of brew did not travel well and was not a particularly refreshing drink when consumed in the heat of the mid-day sun.

By the 1790s, the Bow Brewery had come up with 'Hodgson's India Ale', a lighter beer with a six per cent alcoholic content that was reported to travel well. The ever-thirsty soldiers serving in hot countries were also said to have liked the brew, as it was a more refreshing drink than the earlier beers. Beer drinking abroad had probably grown popular, as it was safer to drink than some of the contaminated water supplies which carried the likelihood of deadly diseases. Another advantage for the brew was the suggestion that it looked more appetising when presented in a bottle as compared to the original darker porters that were displayed in a similar way.

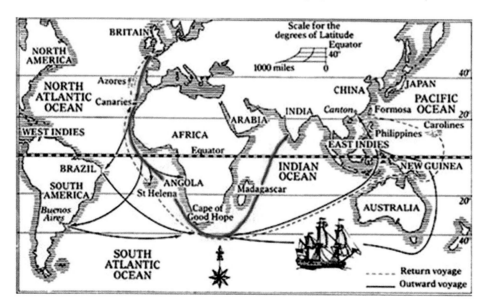

East India Company sailing route

Engraving of Bow Brewery with the old Bow Bridge in foreground

BOW BREWERY.

Painting of Bow Brewery c1827

The development of this new beer was not just an early example of Lea Valley entrepreneurial talent that had allowed Hodgson to exploit a market opportunity through the East India Company. It was also about Hodgson having the necessary skills to identify and select the right ingredients and then to use the available technology to make an appetising brew that travelled well. Who could have guessed that over two hundred years later we would be enjoying a beer that is regularly served in public houses around the world, first dreamed up by George Hodgson at his Bow Brewery that is now more popularly known as IPA (India Pale Ale). It can now be confidently claimed that George Hodgson's IPA was first brewed in London's Lea Valley before it was manufactured at Burton upon Trent.

Should the real aficionados of the amber nectar wish to receive a technical explanation of the various brewing techniques used to produce this tipple, they should refer to the references listed below.

References

Boulton, Christopher, *Encyclopaedia of Brewing*, Wiley-Blackwell (2013)

Oliver, Garrett (editor), *The Oxford Companion to Beer*, Oxford University Press (2011)

Unger, Richard, *Beer in the Middle Ages and the Renaissance*, University of Pennsylvania Press (2004)

THE ABSOLUTELY INCREDIBLE
HARPER TWELVETREES

It is not often, from the distance of the 21st century, that we are allowed the opportunity to look inside the mind of a 19th-century entrepreneur, industrialist and philanthropist, particularly as there are few physical traces, unless one knows where to look, of this remarkable man. This man, Harper Twelvetrees, through his energy, thoughtfulness and morality has set an example, which many of us would find hard to follow. Taking account of the time, the examples he set, although quite revolutionary, may not exactly match our present expected standards of equality. However, some of his initiatives would do credit to many government agencies and employers if they were introduced today. While carrying out research for this chapter I was particularly fortunate in discovering a file of correspondence which has allowed a unique glimpse of a mid-19th century industrial area in the southern part of the Lea Valley.

Harper Twelvetrees was born at Biggleswade in Bedfordshire in December 1823, the son of a local builder. At the age of 14 he was apprenticed in a neighbouring town to the printing, stationery and bookselling trade. When he was only 16 the owner of the firm for which he worked died and Harper was asked to take over the management of the business. For agreeing to this, he was given a share in the firm. While, on the face of it, this seemingly rash decision by the inheritors of the business may have been no more than an expedient, it does show that in a little over two years young Harper had mastered the requisite skills to cope with the task before him. It also suggests that he was considered trustworthy.

Harper stayed with the firm until he was 22 and while there he took the opportunity to educate himself. He would get up early in the morning and spend the time between 3.30am and 5.30am reading and studying. The subjects he studied were wide ranging and covered English literature, ancient and modern history, chemistry and, as he put it, "several of the sciences". It would seem that he had also deliberately tried to strengthen this knowledge by giving lectures to various temperance societies and mechanics' institutes. By 1845, Harper appears to have set up business on his own account in another part of Bedfordshire and it was during this time that his interest in chemistry deepened, a subject that was to have a major influence on his later life.

In 1848 Harper moved to London and went into partnership with the idea of manufacturing a cheap range of products for laundry use, but he soon gave up on the venture. This, he said was because "... the vexatious regulations of the excise in connection with the soap-duties interfered with the full development of that particular branch to which my attention had been directed ...". A little while after the move, in 1849, Harper's wife Mary died.

In 1851 Harper married Isabella Noble and soon afterwards he received a proposal from his father-in-law, John Noble, then Mayor of Boston in Lincolnshire, who, at the time, ran a printing and bookselling business with his son in Market Place. John Noble had wished to retire from the business and he invited Harper to enter into partnership with his son. This Harper did and the partnership lasted four years. In 1853 the duty on soap, which had earlier caused Harper to abandon his manufacturing aspirations, was abolished. Now, Harper had the encouragement he needed to re-evaluate his earlier plans to set up as a manufacturer of cheap laundry products; only this time he was determined to go it alone.

About 1855 Harper Twelvetrees with his second wife, Isabella and now with young son Walter moved from Boston and took up residence at Tudor Grove, Hackney in East London. Shortly afterwards Harper started to manufacture his laundry products at a factory in Goswell Road in the neighbouring borough of Islington. In 1858 Harper moved his business to a larger factory site adjacent to the River Lea in Three Mills Lane at Bromley-by-Bow. As there was living accommodation within the factory complex Harper moved his family onto the site. The house was a detached building having a basement and three stories; each floor had four rooms. There was a garden of about four acres and also a paddock of similar size. Previously the house was said to have been the home of a refugee Huguenot family named Lefevre. It was also said that the house was the birthplace of Shaw-Lefevre (the family name may have been changed to avoid persecution) who later became Speaker of the House of Commons. Shaw-Lefevre (1794-1888), on his retirement as Speaker, was raised to the peerage under the title of Viscount Eversley of Heckford. When Harper moved in to his new residence he decided to name the property, 'Eversley House' after its former tenant.

We are extremely fortunate to have Walter Noble Twelvetrees' (1852-1941) childhood recollections of the house and its surroundings recorded in correspondence in 1932, when he was eighty. Walter recalls that the house "… was evidently old, as all the rooms etc. were panelled. I presume the house stood long ago in the middle of the whole area later occupied by the works and grounds, and may have been a farm house with land extending towards Poplar, long before the railway was built". The River Lea also appears to have made a lasting impression on Walter when he wrote, "… during high spring tides, the gardens of Eversley House were sometimes completely flooded, within a few ft. of the house and I have seen 2 or 3ft. of water in the basement." He also tells us that he did not know when the works were built. However, he explained "… I remember that the various buildings looked old when I first saw them in 1859 or 1860." We again learn from his letters that, "… before 1860, there were three factories to which entrance was gained through the work's gateway. One of these formed the nucleus of Imperial Works [Harper Twelvetrees Manufactory], another was occupied by Messrs. Cleugh, jute manufacturers and the third by Messrs. Hayter, who carried on some process connected with woolly substances, probably the production of shoddy" (this was a fibre made from old cloth and the name has passed into modern language and now refers to anything of poor quality). The railway referred to by Walter formed the southern boundary of the site and was the London Tilbury and Southend line, which crossed the River Lea at the same point as the railway does today.

It should be remembered that at the time thousands of people were dying in London of cholera and typhoid and, as a consequence, this had provoked a massive programme of building new sewers and improvements to the capital's supply of drinking water. Coincidentally, the Abbey Mills pumping station at Stratford, completed in 1868, was located approximately 500 metres to the east of Harper's Imperial Chemical Works. The building was jointly designed by Sir Joseph Bazalgette (an Enfield born man) and Edmund Cooper and formed part of Bazalgette's new London sewage system. Interestingly, when Walter Nobel Twelvetrees recalled his early childhood memories of Bromley-by-Bow (in 1932) he wrote that he remembered the ground to the north of Three Mills Lane was situated behind a long wall that ran the length of the lane and was known as "Farmer Mann's". He further recalled that when the Metropolitan Drainage Works were in progress that there was "... excavating, tunnelling or boring operations in Mann's fields". It is therefore highly likely that young Walter had witnessed part of the construction of Bazalgette's London sewerage network.

Harper Twelvetrees, although being a businessman of considerable vision, drive and opportunity would also appear to have had a caring side. In setting up his factory to manufacture laundry and other products, which were sold in large quantities throughout the old British Empire, he seems to have genuinely wanted to make sure that ordinary working people had access to a range of cheap commodities that would improve their personal hygiene and the cleanliness of their homes. He had commented that he wished to "... encourage cleanliness among the poor by selling them a packet of soap powder for a penny", this would equate to around 0.4 pence today. An article in *Shops and Companies of London*, edited by Henry Mayhew, published circa 1865, describes a visit to the Imperial Chemical Works by an unnamed chronicler. It allows an insight into the range of products manufactured by Harper Twelvetrees, who at the time was employing around 420 people. The reporter writes:

Harper Twelvetrees (1823-1881)

> ... it is impossible to give the reader an adequate idea, other than by stating that there are no less than twelve distinct businesses comprised within one establishment, some of which are kept working night and day, and of which the following are the particulars:

1. A manufactory for the production of "Saponine" and Glycerine Soap Powders, as well as Washing Powders, which is said to be considerably larger than any similar establishment in the world.

2. A manufactory for Laundry Thumb and Blue Ball, Soluble Powder Blue and Liquid Blue.

3. A manufactory for Satin Enamel Starch, and Briggs' Australian Glaze Starch.

4. A manufactory for Blacking, in Paste and Liquid, and Harness Polishing Fluid.

5. A manufactory for Block Blacklead and Powder Lead.

6. A manufactory for Metallic Writing Inks and Marking Inks.

7. A manufactory for Baking and Pastry Powder, Yeastrine, and Egg and Butter Powders.

8. A small Soap Boiling plant for the production of Mottled and Pale Soaps, and a Re-melting plant for Perfumed Toilet Soaps.

9. A Chemical plant for the manufacture of Epsom Salts, and various Fine Chemicals.

10. An extensive grinding and packing business in Spices, Gingers, Rices, and various Miscellaneous Goods usually sold by Grocers in packets.

11. A wholesale business in Drysalters' Goods, Gums, Alum, Soda, Acids, Loogwood, Saltpetre, Brimstone, Twines, Seeds, Etc., Etc.

12. A manufactory fitted with circular saws, lathes, and every requisite for the production of Clothes-Wringing Machines and other Washing Machinery.

From the above list it will be noted that Harper was producing, apart from his laundry goods, packaged food products for the grocery trade and he was also manufacturing products that could be supplied to bakers. Saltpetre could be supplied to butchers as it was used in the curing of meats. It should not be forgotten that in our parents' and grandparents' day ready- meals off-the-shelf and takeaways were unheard of. Most meals for the family were prepared and consumed at home with simple ingredients purchased from a local butcher, milkman, baker and grocer. Many of these tradespeople would rely on manufacturers like Harper Twelvetrees' for their supplies and also local farms for their ingredients. Our ancestors did not have the luxury of refrigeration so food had to be purchased regularly. There were no "best before" or "sell by" dates therefore a throwaway culture did not exist. In general, people did not waste food, they couldn't afford to, and tasty meals were often invented from left-over scraps, making at least one person in the household a reasonable cook.

To give an indication of the total number of products manufactured at the Imperial Chemical Works in a single year, it has been calculated that 101,843,464 labels were used in the identification of each individual item. The success of Harper's business was probably due to the considerable amount of publicity he engaged in which, apart from the individual product labelling, had three strategic advertising strands. First, the general public were made aware of the name Twelvetrees and his products by large letters painted on hoardings and walls, normally white lettering on a blue background to represent the colour of his powders and laundry blue. Second, he would address the reading classes through advertisements in newspapers, magazines and journals and thirdly he would send what were classified as "illuminated show-bills" and trade catalogues to the shops that stocked his goods.

For the day, this degree of advertising was quite radical and occasionally it became the subject of criticism and derision by a few of Harper's non-progressive customers. To them, this form of promotion was nothing less than boasting. One amusing example of this can be seen in the correspondence (23rd September 1864) of a Guildford shopkeeper who returned one of Harper's catalogues with the following remarks:

Engraving of Harper Twelvetrees Imperial Chemical Works, Three Mill Lane, Bromley-by-Bow c1860

Sir, I beg to return the enclosed, as I seldom or ever have to do with puffing houses. Good articles will generally find their way with the public without such nonsense, to say the least of it. Remaining your obedient servant.

Harper's measured response of around eight hundred words is a literary gem and a small part of it is reproduced here to give the reader a flavour of his reply:

Sir, I beg to acknowledge the receipt of your communication of the 23rd September (returning my wholesale catalogue), in which you inform me that you decline to do business with what you are pleased to characterise 'puffing houses'. I must beg of you to excuse me if I remark, that I had imagined that all the tradesmen of your antique stamp had died out long since, not having met with any such during the past twenty-five years that I have been engaged in commercial life. …

History has shown that there is always a minority who will resist new ideas and not wish to embrace change, even if it can be demonstrated that there are future benefits to be had. Fortunately, Harper Twelvetrees appears not to have been too hampered in this respect as an article by the editor of the *Stratford Times* (9th November 1861) shows. The editor begins the piece by first giving a description of Bromley-by-Bow in the following manner:

It was the obscurest of obscure districts, and everything about the place tended to produce upon the mind an impression of stunted powers and dwarfish capabilities. Constituting, as it does, one of the fag-ends of the county of Middlesex, divided from the Essex marshes by the murky Lea (whose easy current forms, amongst other uses for which it is adapted, a main sewer which touches not the pockets of the ratepayers), there was some danger at one time of its being altogether overwhelmed by its more busy and flourishing neighbours, with whom communication was rendered difficult; for every outlet, street, or byway in the place appeared formed upon the most crooked, crazy, and circuitous principle imaginable. …. The smoke and stench arising from gas-factories, tan-works, glass-houses, bone grinders, etc., had blanched the face of vegetation and

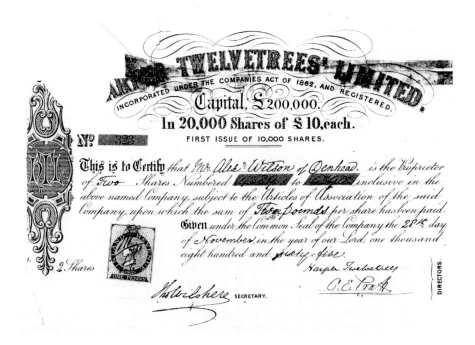

Share certificate issued to Mr Alec Wilson for two shares (£3 paid for each share) in Harper Twelvetrees Limited 28th November 1865

produced a striking anomaly in the market-gardens which once flourished in the neighbourhood.

This rather damning and graphic description of the area goes on much longer, but I am sure that by now the reader will have got the picture! Here, from the *Stratford Times,* we also get a pretty clear account of the market-gardens, which were once prolific in East London, being forced out of the area by industrial pollution. In recognising the polluting effects of industry, the editor really was ahead of his time.

After depicting such a dismal scene and totally condemning the area the editor's article becomes positively up-beat when he explains:

> But lately a great change has been apparent in the neighbourhood. Instead of dirty, narrow lanes bounded by high walls, now there are to be seen neat, commodious, and well-built cottages, flanking tidy roads. The old population is losing its distinctive traits before a new, fresh, and vigorous class that is rapidly settling amongst them, and giving an air of busy life and incessant occupation to a place, which once wore an empty gloom hardly redeemed by the wild rush of waters roaring in the adjacent mill-stream. … One fact, however, must be borne in mind – one which becomes a matter of deep interest and moment, as affording some idea of what may be accomplished by the efforts of an unaided man. The change produced is attributed, to a very large extent, to the influence exercised by a single individual – and that individual is Mr. Harper Twelvetrees.

Harper Twelvetrees, unlike many factory owners of his generation, held the view that his workers would perform their duties better if he provided good working conditions and a number of fringe benefits. While it is always difficult to guess what motivates some bosses to provide decent working conditions for their employees, it is fairly clear that, for Harper Twelvetrees, there were more worthwhile goals in life other than just seeking profit.

Harper had a number of cottages built close to his factory to provide accommodation for his employees and their families. He also set up a lecture hall in a large workshop of a factory previously occupied by Messrs. Hayter (mentioned above) which was now part of his industrial complex. As an indication of Harper's commitment to the region the wider community was allowed to use this facility for concerts

A Tesco supermarket and car park now stands on the site of Harper Twelvetrees factory

SPECIAL PRICE LIST FOR EXPORT & WHOLESALE MERCHANTS.

HARPER TWELVETREES AND SON,

Cordova Works, Grove Road, Bow, London, E.

SOLE MANUFACTURERS OF HARPER TWELVETREES' ORIGINAL PATENT

GLYCERINE SOAP POWDER,

CLEANSING CRYSTALS AND OTHER WASHING POWDERS, BALL BLUE, BLACK LEAD, BAKING POWDER, &c., &c.

Respectfully inform their WHOLESALE and EXPORT CUSTOMERS, that having considerably enlarged their MANUFACTURING PREMISES, they now possess unequalled facilities for the execution of Orders, for a continuance of which they will feel greatly honoured and obliged.

☞ HARPER TWELVETREES & SON'S Export Glycerine Soap Powder is SPECIALLY PREPARED for the climates of Australia, New Zealand, United States, Canada, South Africa, the Mediterranean Ports, and the West Indies. Every Packet guaranteed to be of the same quality as formerly manufactured by HARPER TWELVETREES, the INVENTOR, PATENTEE, and ORIGINAL MANUFACTURER, and to contain FOUR TIMES THE WASHING STRENGTH OF ANY OTHER WASHING POWDER.

HARPER TWELVETREES & SON'S WASHING & SOAP POWDERS.

	Per Gross.
GLYCERINE SOAP POWDER FOR EXPORT } Specially prepared and guaranteed	5/-
LAUNDRY SOAP POWDER, Penny Packets 4oz.	5/6
No. 1 DRY SOAP—Kiln-dried Tallow Soap, 2oz.	5/-
GLYCERISED SOAP POWDER, 2oz.	5/-
ORIGINAL SOAP POWDER, 2oz.	4/-
WASHING & CLEANSING CRYSTALS, 2oz.	3/6
ORIGINAL WASHING POWDER, (not Soap Powder) 2oz.	3/6
ECONOMICAL SOAP POWDER, 6oz. very large	7/-
DRY SOAP, in 4oz. & 8oz. Tinfoil Packets, 28/- per cwt.	

HARPER TWELVETREES & SON'S Pure & Genuine Baking Powders.

First Manufactured by HARPER TWELVETREES in 1848.

No. 1, Best Baking and Pastry Powder, in Bottles for EXPORTATION, various sizes	
Shilling Canisters	6/6 per doz.
Sixpenny "	3/9 "
Penny Packets	6/- per gross.
No. 2, Superior Baking Powder:—	
Penny Packets	5/- per gross.
Sixpenny Canisters	3/6 per doz.
Shilling "	6/- "
No. 3, Economical Baking Powder:—	
Penny Packets	4/- per gross.
Smaller Packets	2/9 "

RICE STARCH.

In 5lb. papers, Best Quality	30/- per cwt.
In 4oz., 8oz., and 16oz., packets	34/- "
In 2oz.	36/- "
No. 1 LONDON RICE STARCH in papers, 28/-	"
DOUBLE REFINED POWDER STARCH, green label, 2oz., 4oz., 8oz., and 16oz.	
7lb. papers	32/- "

HARPER TWELVETREES & SON'S LAUNDRY BALL BLUE.

Is unequalled in any market for Quality at the price. COMPARE SAMPLES.

In 1oz. and ½oz. Balls, 4 and 7lb. boxes	40/- per cwt.
Very Brilliant Quality	46/- "
If ½oz. & ¼ Balls 2/- extra. If 1lb. and 2lb. boxes 2/6 more.	
FAMILY Sixpenny boxes	45/- per gross.

INDIGO THUMB & LION BLUE.

In ¼oz. ½oz. and 1oz. Thumbs or Cakes, at 7d., 8d., 9d.,

BLACK LEADS IN POWDER.

PURE PENCIL LEAD, Æ Quality the finest imported, 1oz., 4oz., and 8oz. packets ... 40/- per cwt.
Packed in TINFOIL for Exportation.

No. 1, Pencil Lead in green label	30/-	"
" 2, " superior	24/-	"
" 3, " Red Labels	18/-	"
" 4, Servants' Friend, White Labels	15/-	"

Customers' name and address on Labels for 1cwt. each size.

BLOCK BLACK LEAD.

NICKEL SILVER (Registered) BLACK LEAD, in 1oz., 2oz., and 4oz. blocks	5/-	per box.
PURE PENCIL LEAD, Æ quality	40/-	per cwt.
No. 1, Ditto	30/-	"
" 2, Ditto superior	24/-	"
" 3, Ditto in 7lb. papers	18/-	"
BALL BLACK LEAD	24/-	"

SCENTED HAIR OIL, RED OR PALE.

Sixpenny Bottles	4/-	per dozen.
Shilling ditto	7/-	"
Large ditto ... 10/- 12/- and 14/-		"
Loose, in Casks or Tins	5/6	per gallon.

WRITING INKS.

BLACK, Penny Glass Bottles, various shapes, capsuled,
5/- per gross.
" " sealed 4/6 "
" SIX-PENNY stone bottles 2/9 per doz.
" SHILLING " Pint bottles 5/6 "
BLUE, Penny Glass Bottles ... 5/- per gross.

MISCELLANEOUS.

EPSOM SALTS, 1oz. packets, 7lb. boxes, per cwt.
" " Loose in casks "
CARBONATE OF SODA, 1oz. packets, 7lb. boxes "
" " Loose in casks "
CARBONATE OF MAGNESIA, 1d. packets 7/- per gross
CREAM OF TARTAR, 1oz., and in penny packets.
SENNA LEAVES, ½d. packets, 3/6 per gross, and penny packets, 6/- per gross.
FLOUR OF SULPHUR, 1oz., 2oz., 4oz. 24/- per cwt
MILK OF SULPHUR, 1d. packets, 7lb. boxes.
VENETIAN RED, 2oz., and 4oz. ... 14/- "
ROTTEN STONE, best 2oz., and 4oz., 14/- "
TARTARIC ACID, (English make) powdered in casks.
GUM ARABIC, Loose, 9d. per pound and upwards.
NURSERY VIOLET POWDER, penny packets and quarter gross boxes, 5/- per gross.
PREPARED FULLERS EARTH, penny packets, and quarter gross boxes. 5/- per gross.

Part of a price list issued by Harper Twelvetrees after his discharge as a bankrupt. Note new address.

and "select and popular entertainments". To improve the education of local people he provided the lecture hall with a well-stocked library and also arranged evening classes for adults. In 1862 a "sick and benevolent fund" was set up and all those joining the Imperial Chemical Works had to contribute one hour's pay each week. Members in need of relief were paid weekly in accordance with a graduated table based on the amount of contribution paid in. Once a year there was a meeting of the fund holders and any surplus that had accrued was paid back to the members in proportion to their contributions. The workers also enjoyed the facilities of a "clothing club" and a "penny savings bank" and on the leisure side the factory had its own brass band, a drum and fife band and a cricket club.

On Sundays the hall was used for religious worship and the preaching was said to be non-sectarian on account of "Christian ministers of all denominations having conducted the services". A Bible class was held on Sunday afternoon "for the religious instruction of such young men as are disposed to seek it". No doubt considered politically correct at the time, "Mothers' Sewing Meetings" were held "for the improvement of the women in the locality".

On the 4th November 1861, when the lecture hall officially opened, addresses were given by Acton S. Ayrton, MP, the Sheriffs of London and Middlesex and John Cassell, the Rector of Bow. It was further reported that dignitaries came from all over the country to congratulate Harper Twelvetrees for his philanthropic contribution to the community. While more research is required to confirm, beyond doubt, the names of the prominent speakers who attended the regular meetings, held at what became known as the Institute, there is evidence to suggest that internationally famous people such as Robert Todd Lincoln (1843-1926) (son of President Abraham Lincoln and the last United States Minister to Britain before the title changed to Ambassador), John Stuart Mill (1806-1873) (British philosopher and economist), John Bright (1811-1889) (British reformer and free trade advocate) and Lord Shaftesbury (Anthony Ashley Cooper, 1801-1885) (social reformer and champion of Factory Acts and Mines Act) had all lectured there.

Bromley-by-Bow, a tiny East London district, was probably not the first place that would spring to mind as a platform for the great 19th-century reformers. However, it would not seem unreasonable to believe that Harper Twelvetrees, FRSL, President of the Bromley Literary Association, member of the London Emancipation Committee and associated with a host of other important bodies, would not have attracted the great and the good to the area, particularly when taking into account his high-profile philanthropic image and flare for advertising. The need to promote the Institute and to communicate to the outside world the benefits of working at the Imperial Chemical Works had not been overlooked either. This was done through the *Bromley Lecture-hall Chronicle*, a publication that journalists often used to supplement their articles.

In 1865, after only seven years in business at Three Mills Lane, with all the attended fanfare and publicity surrounding the product range and what might arguably be described as a genuine passion to improve the lives of working people, Harper Twelvetrees put his Imperial Chemical Works up for sale. The business and premises were sold to a limited company for £53,852-8s-5d and in the following year the General Trading Company Limited purchased the business. At some point Harper appears to have moved to Dublin. According to the reported Court records, under Adjourned Sittings for Examination and Discharge, 24th November 1868, the General Trading Company Limited was in the process of liquidation and as a consequence Harper Twelvetrees has been declared bankrupt. He had only been paid £791- 5s of the agreed purchase money for the Imperial Chemical Works.

When granting the order of discharge, the Judge observed that, "... the Bankrupt was entitled to great sympathy on account of his severe losses, and that it must always be a matter of great regret to find a person who, from a position of affluence, had fallen through his connection with Public Companies. The Bankrupt had assisted his Assignees to the extent of his ability, and had given his evidence very satisfactory, and the order of discharge would be granted." No doubt many in this position would have called it a day, not so Harper Twelvetrees who was about to show the world the meaning of the words morality and determination.

We pick up the threads of the story once more from a "special price list for export and wholesale merchants", published by the newly formed business of Harper

Twelvetrees and Son, Cordova Works, Grove Road, Bow, London, East and begin to piece together the jigsaw. Interestingly, a paragraph has been included at the foot of the price list entitled, *"An Explanation"*. The paragraph is in the form of a communication to Harper's present and former customers, setting out the reasons why he became bankrupt. When reading his account and noting that Harper had apparently the confidence to go into print about the unfortunate episode of his demise, this might indicate that the liquidators had shabbily treated him. In the text Harper explained to his customers that, "… not having been paid by the Company for [his] Business, (except £791-5s on account of the purchase) [he] then offered to take back his Property, and release all claims on the Company. That offer was, however, refused by the Liquidators, who transferred to one of their personal Friends the valuable property which Harper Twelvetrees had accumulated by unremitting toil and anxiety of several years, and for which only the above nominal sum had been paid to him by the Company – thus leaving Harper Twelvetrees at liberty to re-establish himself in Business in his own name, without infringing the rights of any individual whatever."

While Harper's financial state would have been a strong and motivating influence to tempt him back into business, from what we have so far learned of the man it would be difficult to imagine that purely money or personal gain was the sole reason for his decision to return. An evening meeting arranged by Harper's professional acquaintances and friends, and held at Radley's Hotel, Blackfriars, to celebrate his return to business, supports this notion. During the evening's proceedings "numerous congratulatory letters from various wholesale City firms, provincial merchants and absent friends were read …" and the chairman referred to Harper's "… laborious efforts on behalf of the moral, social, intellectual and religious welfare of the working classes". Having the support of so many former customers, business and community acquaintances might indicate that Harper was in the process of making good any outstanding debts that had accrued from the sale of his former business. Being discharged from bankruptcy would have meant that all Harper's debts would have been written off. We may never know the real reason why Harper returned to resurrect his former business and we can only speculate on the likely reasons. For example, he may have wished to make a moral contribution by making good any losses his suppliers might have suffered when he did not receive the agreed amount for his business (it is possible that he was relying on the sale of his business to clear invoices for material received et cetera.). On the other hand, it could have been more a case of wishing to see his once prosperous company back on its feet and trading again. Whatever the reasons, apart from trying to make good his personal losses, as a discharged bankrupt there was no legal requirement to take the action he did.

Harper Twelvetrees Will, made on the 9th October 1881, tells us that he was living at 223 Evering Road, Upper Clapton, Middlesex (now in the London borough of Hackney). A second address, 80 Finsbury Pavement, in the City of London (recorded in the Will) would suggest that this was a business address, probably the company office. From the letterhead of a 1932 communication, it was revealed that a company bearing the name Harper Twelvetrees Ltd, Makers of the "Villa" Washing and Mangling Machines was in operation at 24 City Road, Finsbury Square, London, EC1, but it would appear that his son Walter Noble was not involved in the business.

Harper Twelvetrees died prematurely in November 1881 at the age of 58, only a month after writing his will. His early death has deprived us of learning more about the man. Had he lived to a reasonable age, one might speculate that, we may have seen an autobiography from a man who, after all, was the President of the Bromley Literary Association. However, this early research into Harper Twelvetrees's life has alerted readers in the 21st century to the unfinished story of this truly remarkable man. Having set up his business in London's lower Lea Valley, we have seen, through a combination of philanthropy and humanity that Harper Twelvetrees was able to change radically the social and economic conditions that existed in the impoverished area of 19th century Bromley-by-Bow. From such beginnings one would have expected the area to have gone from strength to strength. Sadly, little remains today as a memorial to Harper's humanity.

References

Author unknown, article from *Stratford Times* (9th November 1861)

Lewis, Jim, *London's Lea Valley, Britain's Best Kept Secret,* Phillimore & Co. Ltd, Chichester (1999)

Mayhew, Henry (editor), *Shops and Companies of London,* Richard Barrett, London

Mew, Elizabeth (the great great granddaughter of Harper Twelvetrees), a personal conversation (February 2000), and the loan of family material.

Tower Hamlets Local History Library, Tower Hamlets, London (file containing correspondence and newspaper cuttings on Harper Twelvetrees and the Imperial Chemical Works)

Appendix

Harper Twelvetrees was deeply involved in helping to promote the plight of a runaway American slave, Jack Burton, and, through The British and Foreign Anti-Slavery Society brought Burton to England.

Jack Burton (born about 1830-1831) was the slave of a plantation owner, Moses Burton of Fayette, Missouri. Not long after he was born Jack's father managed to escape from his owner. Later, when Jack was about seven his mother was sold to a slave trader and the lad effectively became an orphan. Young Jack was befriended by the plantation owner's wife and while growing up he appears to have become proficient in most of the jobs around the estate.

In December 1850 Jack married Marie Tomlin, a slave who lived close to the Burton estate. She had two children from a previous marriage and in their short time together Marie and Jack were to have a child of their own. Less than three years after their marriage, in August 1853, Jack was sold for $1,000 to a farmer in Slaine County, Missouri. Slaves, under the law, were the property of their masters and his owner forbade Jack to see his wife and child. However, Jack nurtured ideas of escape to Canada, at the time part of the British Empire, but before doing so he secretly and illegally visited his wife to tell her of his plan.

While escaping Jack, now with a reward on his head for capture, was pursued and eventually apprehended by a local farmer Seneca Diggs, and in the ensuing struggle Diggs was killed. In about September 1853, with the help of abolitionists, Jack finally made it to Canada. There he settled in Windsor and eventually got work as a plasterer and a labourer. To escape identification as a fugitive, he adopted the name of John Anderson.

In 1854 the American Government requested Anderson's extradition, but Lord Elgin, the Governor General of British North America, would not issue the warrant. However, in April 1860, a local magistrate jailed Anderson on a charge of murder but his release was secured by a Hamilton attorney, Samuel Freeman. Anderson was sent to prison again in October 1860 on a warrant issued by a three-magistrate court after it had received sworn affidavits from persons in Missouri. The charge was again murder. Supported by local abolitionists, Anderson's lawyers, in January 1861, obtained a writ of *habeas corpus* from the Court of Queen's Bench in London. In Canada this action was looked upon as an act of interference. However, before the writ could be served in Canada, Anderson's lawyers had appealed to the Court of Common Pleas in Toronto and Chief Justice William Draper, on 16th February 1861, discharged Anderson on what was essentially a technicality, in that the warrant from the magistrate's court had not actually accused Anderson of murder. The whole episode became a major issue in British-American relations.

John Anderson, an escaped slave helped by Harper Twelvetrees

Anderson was invited to England by The British and Foreign Anti-Slavery Society arriving in the country about June 1861. A celebratory meeting welcoming Anderson to England, chaired by Harper Twelvetrees, was held at Exeter Hall, London.

The meeting was attended by many prominent people including Members of Parliament, leading Quakers and Clergy of different denominations and several made speeches from the platform in praise of Anderson.

Between July and September 1861, John Anderson fulfilled invitations to speak at about 25 meetings, mainly in London and southern England. In December 1861 he enrolled at the British Training Institution at Corby, Northamptonshire where he remained for one year. On the 24th December 1861 he set sail for the Republic of Liberia and, to date, nothing appears to be known of his fate. Fortunately, while in England, he must have been interviewed at some length by Harper Twelvetrees as in 1863 a book was published, edited by Harper, *The Story of the Life of John Anderson, the Fugitive Slave*.

References

Reinders, Robert, *Dictionary of Canadian Biography Online*, University of Toronto (2000)

Twelvetrees, Harper, *The Story of the Life of John Anderson, the Fugitive Slave*, William Tweedie, London (1863)

THE LEA VALLEY'S KEW GARDENS

The story that is about to unfold concerns a remarkable 18th-century medical man whose passion for plant collecting has affected the lives of all of us in the 21st century. This he has done through his interest in discovering plants that could have medicinal and dietary benefits.

The Royal Botanical Gardens at Kew in Southwest London were founded in 1759. They developed out of the plant collection of Princess Augusta, widow of Frederick, Prince of Wales and daughter-in-law of George II. Under the influence of the renowned botanist, Sir Joseph Banks, who had accompanied Captain James Cook on his first voyage to the Pacific (1768-1771), the gardens were increased in size after more exotic plants were acquired. In 1840, the garden, which by now had become world famous was given to the state.

However, there were other botanical gardens (sometimes compared with Kew) in the lower Lea valley in West Ham. These gardens were the result of Dr John Fothergill's great passion for the study and collecting of plants, which appears to have begun in earnest once he had established his medical practice.

John Fothergill was born on 8th March 1712 in a small stone farmhouse at Carr End, Wensleydale, Yorkshire, the second son of John Fothergill, a Quaker. When he was 16 he was apprenticed to an apothecary at Bradford, Yorkshire. To further his chosen profession, Fothergill became a student at Edinburgh University in 1734. While there he attracted the attention of the eminent professor of anatomy, Alexander Monro, who encouraged the young man to train as a physician. Forthergill took Monro's advice and in August 1736 he graduated, after which he spent a further two years as St Thomas's Hospital in London taking a course in medical practice under Sir Edward Wilmot. Interestingly we learn, from Fothergill's biographer, that the journey from Edinburgh to London took between six to nine days and was made by sea.

During his time of study at St Thomas's Fothergill took it upon himself to read books on chemistry, botany and travel. In 1740, with his studies behind him, he made a short tour of Europe with a group of friends, returning in the same year to take up residence at 2 White Hart Court in the City of London where he set up as a physician.

Dr John Fothergill purchased Upton House in West Ham in 1762. The house was demolished in 1872

During his training at St Thomas's Hospital he had become acquainted with many poor people and it was they who sought him out when he set up in practice. To attend to the medical needs of these people, Fothergill often travelled across London, taking no fee for his services. While it is probably fair to say that Fothergill acted out of a genuine sense of kindness, it is also the case that these acts of charity were a mark of his Quaker upbringing. It has been suggested by Fothergill's biographer, R. Hingston Fox, MD that he gained considerable medical experience from these frequent acts of generosity and a saying, "I climbed on the backs of the poor to the pockets of the rich" has been attributed to Fothergill's reward for his charitable endeavours. This, in a way, helps us to understand something of the character of this remarkable man.

Dr John Fothergill (1712-1780)

In 1744 Fothergill was admitted to the College of Physicians and by the age of 36 he had become one of the most respected practitioners in his field. Also, at about this time, he had established one of the largest practices in London. Fothergill also took a great interest in and made a study of some of the more serious diseases that claimed the lives of Londoners, particularly those of children. This led him to conclude that the treatments of the day, normally bleeding and purging, were, in general, harmful to the patient. He therefore developed other less intrusive regimes, some in which he used a preparation of cinchona bark (from which we get quinine). These particular treatments were said to have had successful outcomes for his patients. In 1748 he published *An Account of the Sore-throat attended with Ulcers*. The book gained a wide readership and several editions were published, making him a much sought after consultant for this specialised subject. Further prestige was gained when, in 1754, he was elected fellow of his old college in Edinburgh and further honours came in 1763 and 1776 when he was elected Fellow of the Royal Society (FRS) and fellow of the Royal Society of Medicine at Paris, respectively.

In 1762 Fothergill purchased Upton House in West Ham along with about 30 acres of land, from an Admiral Elliot. Later, land adjacent to the estate was acquired and the gardens surrounding the house were enlarged. Here begins another remarkable chapter in the life of Doctor John Fothergill. The grounds of Upton House became today's West Ham Park, which is one of the many open spaces, including Epping Forest, that is managed by the Corporation of London.

Shortly after he had moved to Upton House and only a little over two years after the foundation of the botanical gardens at Kew, Fothergill had begun to establish his own botanical gardens around his new home. It would appear that Fothergill did not just wish to develop his botanical gardens out of self-interest, nor purely as a means of collecting plants and shrubs for their intrinsic beauty, personal pleasure and fragrance. He wished to introduce new species that might be used as the basis for new medicines and also for sources of food.

Fothergill introduced, what was, for the day, leading edge technology when greenhouses and hothouses were built adjacent to Upton House. The largest of these was a hothouse measuring some 260 feet (80 metres) in length, in which he grew oranges and other tropical fruits. In all some 3,400 different species of trees, plants and shrubs were collected and introduced into the gardens of Upton House. Fothergill's methods of enhancing his collection were quite imaginative. He approached ships' captains at the nearby London Docks and arranged with them to bring back barrels of earth and large interesting rocks as ballast from their overseas voyages. In many cases the barrels of earth also contained stowaways, in the form of seeds, which by accident had found the perfect way of being transported to Britain.

However, Fothergill did not rely solely on this method to procure his plants. He also corresponded with people throughout the world and obtained plants and seeds from places as far away as China and the West Indies. Collectors were employed to search the valleys and forests of North America while others were sent to West Africa. Some he had scouring the Central European Alps in search of specimens for his newly created rock garden. It is claimed that the rock garden at Upton House was the first of its kind in Britain.

Sir Joseph Banks, by this time one of Britain's leading botanists, was so impressed with Fothergill's work that he decided to write, alluding to the great care and attention that had been given to the plant collection, in G. Thompson's, *Memoirs of Fothergill.* Here Banks expressed the view that:

> At an expense seldom undertaken by an individual and with an ardour that was visible in the whole of his conduct, he procured from all parts of the world a great number of the rarest plants, and protected them in the amplest buildings which this or any other country has seen.

He also went on to write, with obvious enthusiasm, that the collection was:

> Equalled by nothing but royal munificence, bestowed upon the botanic gardens at Kew. In my opinion no other garden in Europe, royal or of a subject had nearly so many scarce and valuable plants.

Fothergill, through his plant collecting, had made many friends in America and had developed a great respect, as a libertarian, for the people of these British Colonies. The mainly Quaker colonists of Pennsylvania, some who had descended from William Penn, were opposed, through their religious beliefs, to war and were refusing to pay taxes, levied by Britain, for its prosecution. This along with other disputes over trade and taxes had grown during the 1750s and 1770s and tensions between Britain and its America colonies were steadily mounting. In 1757, Benjamin Franklin, printer, author, diplomat, philosopher and scientist was sent to London by the Pennsylvanian Assembly to petition King George II over these matters. After carrying out his duties Franklin remained in Britain for five years, returning to America in 1762. In 1764, with tensions still running high between the two countries, Franklin again came to Britain as a representative of

Rock Garden West Ham Park, created in the style that Fothergill might have used

the Pennsylvanian Assembly. During the following 11 years of his residence in Britain, Franklin made many close friends. One of these was Doctor Fothergill, who not only attended him as a physician but also became intimately involved in discussions with Franklin over the best possible ways of creating a breakthrough that would reduce tensions and solve the political differences between the two countries.

In his later years the demands on Fothergill as a physician and also his other work kept him away from his beloved botanical gardens. Management of the estate at Upton House was left to his 15 gardeners. Occasionally he would come by coach at night to visit the gardens and view his plants by lantern. Fothergill died in 1780 and was buried at the Friends Burial Ground in Winchmore Hill, North London. The headstone that once marked his grave has been removed and the caretaker in charge of the Burial Ground told the author that it was taken to Ackworth School in Yorkshire, an establishment that Fothergill had founded.

Upton House was renamed Ham House and was eventually acquired by the Gurney family, the well-known philanthropic Quakers. In 1872 Ham House was demolished and Fothergill's rock garden removed. After a petition from the people of West Ham to the Corporation of London to raise funds for the preservation of the land as an open space, sufficient capital was raised (with a generous donation from the Gurneys) to open, in 1874, what we now know as West Ham Park. A stone kern, constructed with material said to be from Ham House and Fothergill's rock garden, now stands in the park close to the site of the original house.

Fortunately, during Fothergill's lifetime he had commissioned several famous artists to draw, paint and record his plants, trees and shrubs. After Fothergill's death, Catherine the Great, Empress of Russia, purchased approximately twelve hundred of these pictures for £2,300, which, by today's standards, would equate to several million pounds. Until recently, the pictures had remained forgotten and unseen since their acquisition in 1781.

In the late 1980s, the Chief Curator of the Komorov Botanical Library in St Petersburg discovered a large quantity of Fothergill's pictures still in their original wrapping. The author has been privileged to see a small selection of photographs

The former Superintendent of West Ham Park, David Jones CBE, standing next to stone cairn close to the site where Upton House once stood

that were taken of these pictures and has been genuinely astounded by their quality and exquisite colouring. In 2002 negotiations to bring the collection back to Britain, to have delicate restoration work completed, had been put in place. The paper that was used for their production was in a poor state of preservation. Once restoration work has been completed it is hoped to put the collection on public display. This would provide a fitting memorial to Doctor John Fothergill, a most remarkable man, who, through his love of plants, has been able to bring beauty into our lives long after his death.

The author was extremely fortunate to be given a private tour of the gardens in West Ham Park by their most knowledgeable Superintendent, David Jones CBE just before he retired from his position in 2002. Mr Jones pointed out a Maidenhair Tree (Ginko biloba) that had been planted in 1763, during Fothergill's time at Upton House. The tree had apparently flowered, for the first time, sixteen years after Fothergill's death when it was 33 feet (ten metres) tall. Mr Jones explained that the tree had been planted against the front wall of the former Upton House so that it could attract maximum sunshine and also warmth from the adjacent brickwork. A careful study of its trunk showed a flattened area that had presumably been shaped by the tree's close proximity to the building.

During Mr Jones's time at West Ham Park he had carried out a programme of restoration and had also re-introduced a rock garden along with other plants and shrubs that had previously been grown by Fothergill. On the day of the author's visit (13th February 2002) a re-introduced tea tree plant had bloomed for the first time. This made the plant the first of its species to have bloomed in the gardens since Fothergill's day.

We should all be eternally grateful to those early pioneers like Dr John Fothergill who had the foresight, courage and determination to experiment with growing and cultivating unusual plants that were not native to this country. In this way he has helped to increase our botanists and horticulturalists understanding of ways that new plant species are propagated. In the longer term this has enabled growers to implement the cultivation of nutritious fruit and vegetables on a large scale. The benefits to health derived from such knowledge have proved a lifeline for millions of people around the world and the results are truly immeasurable, particularly if breakthroughs in the beneficial uses of certain types of plants and medicines that are derived from them are taken into account.

References

Author unknown, *Catherine the Great's lost Botanical Drawings*, Cardington

Fox, R. Hingston, *Dr. John Fothergill and his Friends*, Macmillan & Co. Ltd, London (1919)

Jones, David, interview (February 2002)

Lee, Sidney (editor), *Dictionary of National Biography*, Smith Elder & Co. (1909)

Lewis, Jim, *East Ham & West Ham Past*, Historical Publications Ltd, London (2004)

Powell, W.R., *The Victoria History of the County of Essex, Vol. 6*, Oxford University Press (1973)

EARLY AGRICULTURE AND HORTICULTURE IN THE LEA VALLEY

Most people would probably believe that the Lea Valley region is famous only for its plethora of world changing industrial and scientific firsts, but that would be a false assumption. The truth is the Lea Valley has a long and proud association with both horticulture and agriculture and this actively encouraged a range of supporting industries and service providers to develop and set up in the region.

Referring to the Domesday Book it can be seen that there was considerable farming and smallholding activity in the area as our distant ancestors began to learn the skills and techniques of planting and husbandry which helped to support and sustain a growing population.

It is hard to imagine that an area like today's Newham, with its rapidly changing skyline and the borough that hosted the 2012 Olympics and Paralympics, was growing potatoes on a commercial scale from the early 18th century. To help with the harvesting of the crop, Irish labour had to be imported to lift and collect the tubers which were becoming an important part of the daily diet of people in Britain.

Growing vegetables was fairly common in East London at the turn of the 20th century and areas of cultivation seemed to crop up (pardon the pun) in the most unlikely places. During the 19th century, the fundamentals of agriculture were taught to the two hundred boys of St Edward's Roman Catholic Reformatory School on the 14 acres of land attached to the school building – Green Street House, East Ham. This agricultural land was the former home of West Ham United Football Club that has recently moved to its new home on Queen Elizabeth Park.

We have seen in the chapter *The Lea Valley's Kew Gardens* that the Quaker, Dr John Fothergill (1712-1780) purchased Upton House in West Ham (now Newham) in 1762 and set up home and also his doctor's practice. Here, in the grounds of his house (now West Ham Park) he established a botanical garden which, at the time rivalled the Royal Botanical Gardens at Kew. Apart from growing exotic fruit and plants in hot houses that he had built, he planted shrubs and trees from around the world that could be used as a basis for new medicines and also food. Astonishingly his plant collection amounted to over 3,400 different species.

Botanical Gardens, Madeira, one of the many places supplied by Loddiges of Hackney

Botanical Gardens, Madeira

Green Street House West Ham known as Boleyn Castle. West Ham United took out a lease on the site in 1904

In the 1740s, Johann Busch (anglicised to John Busch or John Bush) arrived in Hackney from Germany and became a supplier of unusual plants to several botanical gardens and in particular to those of Princess Augusta, daughter-in-law of George II. Augusta's plant collection was to eventually form the basis for the Royal Botanic Gardens at Kew. Busch's work appears to have got him noticed and he was invited to Russia by Catherine the Great and commissioned to lay out gardens in the "English-style".

Not long after Busch, in the early 1760s, another German Joachim Conrad Loddiges, a gardener, settled in Hackney. After working to landscape the grounds of Dr (later Sir) John Baptist Silvester he set up in business as an importer of rare seeds and plants. Many of these he cultivated in large steam heated hot houses that he had built on a site in Mare Street, Hackney approximately where the Town Hall stands today. When hardy, many of these plants were exported overseas in special packaging which Loddiges had designed.

Engraving of Green Street House known as Boleyn Castle

In the early 19th century, plants from the Loddiges nursery were sent to Madeira where they helped to establish a successful tea plantation on the island. As the popularity of the Loddiges nursery grew, plants were supplied to the royal parks and also to the great estates of Woburn Abbey and Chatsworth. When the building used for the Great Exhibition of 1851 was relocated (in 1854) from Hyde Park to the site at Crystal Palace, Sydenham, a massive Mauritius fan palm weighing around 15 tons left the Loddiges Nursery to adorn the building, making its way by road to its new destination pulled by 32 horses.

Joachim Conrad Loddiges
(1738-1826)

As the 19th century progressed the march of industry continued, fuelled by the expansion of the railways, and pressure across East London mounted for sites to build new factories and also houses for the rapidly growing population that had been attracted to the area by the promise of work. This made smallholding and nursery land an obvious target for the developers and as the factories took hold in the lower Lea Valley, they caused increased levels of atmospheric pollution and also severe poisoning of water courses (see a reference to this by the editor of the *Stratford Times*, in an article, 9th November 1861, in the chapter about Harper Twelvetrees). As might be imagined this made the area less favourable to growers and it became a case of either closing down or moving out. The attraction of cheaper land in the cleaner environment of the upper Lea Valley made districts like Enfield, Waltham Cross, Waltham Abbey, Cheshunt and Nazeing ideal places for established and new growers to put down their roots. There was also the added attraction that the London markets were only a horse and cart journey away.

From the beginning of the 19th century a number of small nurseries had set up in the region of the upper Lea Valley. According to the late Peter Rooke, whose grandfather George had run nurseries in the Lea Valley, these were little more than open patches of ground where vegetables and bedding plants were grown out of doors. By the end of the century, with pressure on the lower Lea Valley growers to move due to the clamour of industry for building land, it had become clear that the upper Lea Valley offered the best opportunities for those who wished to start again.

The former ground of West Ham United once stood on the site of St Edward's Reformatory School where some 200 boys received agriculture training

Loddiges' hothouse, claimed to be the largest in the world at the time

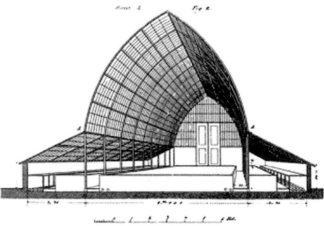

As the upper Lea Valley growers' businesses had no doubt been drawn to this part of the region by its fertile loams and abundant water supplies, the area must have looked extremely attractive to those who were being forced out of areas of London polluted by industry which had a long way to go before it came under tight legally enforceable environmental controls. With the lower region's growers moving into the area alongside their upper Lea Valley counterparts it would have probably seemed obvious to these early pioneers that as their numbers increased, they could collectively become a dominant force in Britain's horticultural industry. However, for this to happen, the growers would need to come together as an organised group.

As we will learn in a later chapter, on Tuesday 31st October 1911 a meeting of representatives from the Nurserymen and Growers of the Lea Valley was convened at the Imperial Club, Waltham Cross when a resolution was moved by the Chairman and passed by those attending: "That an Association be formed which shall be called 'The Lea Valley and District Nurserymen's and Growers' Association". This organisation is known today as The Lea Valley Growers' Association which produces large quantities of tomatoes, peppers, aubergines, salad leaf and cucumbers for the British grocery market.

References

Lewis, Jim, *London's Lea Valley Britain's Best Kept Secret,* Phillimore & Co. Ltd, Chichester (1999)

Lewis, Jim, *East Ham & West Ham Past*, Historical Publications Ltd, London (2004)

Lewis, Jim, *A Century of Growing the History of the Lea Valley Growers' Association from 1911 to 2011*, Libri Publishing Ltd, London (2011)

STRATFORD LANGTHORNE ABBEY

Looking at Stratford today it is almost impossible to imagine that the area was once open marshland stretching towards the Thames. It is probably even more difficult to imagine a group of Cistercian monks building a monastery here. The monastery, begun in the twelfth century, was to become known as the Abbey of Stratford Langthorne, or, more familiarly, West Ham Abbey.

Abbot Robert, who had become increasingly uncomfortable with the growing wealth and power of the Benedictines, led 21 monks away from his monastery at Molesmes in France and founded the Cistercian order in 1098 at Citeaux, east of Dijon. Although scholars have differed with regard to the figures, it would seem that within one hundred years of founding their order the Cistercians had established around eight hundred abbeys across Europe. Research has shown that the order established their communities near fertile ground usually away from areas of high population. This would suggest that, at the time when West Ham Abbey was being built, Stratford was a relatively isolated and sparsely populated place. The Domesday survey of 1086 tells us that the population of the area, which later became known as West Ham comprised 48 villagers, 79 smallholders and three slaves.

From old maps and documents, it can be deduced that the Abbey occupied a site of approximately 20 acres and was situated east of the Channelsea River and west of Manor Road (formerly Marsh Lane). Travellers approaching London from the east could not have failed to see what must have been a massive building silhouetted against the skyline. By the time of the dissolution of the monasteries between 1536 and 1540 by Henry VIII, the site had grown to accommodate mills, kilns,

Cistercian monk. It now is hard to imagine, that once this order founded an abbey in Stratford

Abbey Gardens, Stratford, a community garden on the site of the old Abbey of Stratford Langthorne

Window arches from abbey now in the porch of All Saints Church, West Ham

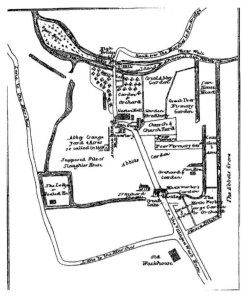

Katherine Fry's map

orchards, gardens, moated areas, a tanning house, a slaughterhouse, a bake house, a church, and various other buildings. So, it can be seen that, over the years, the monks had created a self-sustaining community. To accomplish this level of self-sufficiency the Cistercians had developed a sound economic model to ensure that the day-to-day tasks of running the monastery were carried out efficiently. This was achieved by creating a two-tier system of monks and in today's terminology it would probably be classified as a division of labour. Lay brothers were admitted to the monastery; but they were not required to carry out spiritual duties. Their functions were purely the management and running of the agricultural, commercial and industrial side of the community. Without this division of labour, it would have been almost impossible to have produced sufficient food and drink to sustain a flourishing monastery up until the time of the reformation.

References

Author unknown, *The Big Dig, Archaeology and the Jubilee Line Extension*, Museum of London Archaeology Service, London (1998)

Evans, F.T., *Monastic Multinationals: the Cistercians and other Monks as Engineers, Vol. 68*, the Newcomen Society (1996-7)

Fry, Katherine, (edited by G. Pagen), *History of the Parish of East & West Ham*, London (1888)

The great gate of the abbey (18th-century engraving)

Katherine Fry's drawing of Abbey Mills

AN ANCIENT WHISKY DISTILLERY
IN THE LEA VALLEY

Over the years, when researching industrial history stories, particularly in the lower Lea Valley the author has often found references or picked up interesting snippets of information in various archives about subjects outside his area of research. One such was a reference to a whisky distillery when beginning research for this book it was not clear if the whisky distillery story was a figment of the author's imagination. An email to a great source of local information, Richard Durack, of the Newham Local Studies Library & Archives, revealed that the whisky distillery story was not some aberration of an ageing historian's mind, which was quite reassuring to know, as he kindly passed on information which has allowed further study.

Consulting the Kelly's Directory of Essex for 1882 we come across the first listing of Phillips & Brock, whisky distillers, Warton Road, Stratford. In the Directory of 1891/92, the business had become listed as the Lea Valley Distillery Company. Later, in 1892/93, the company is still listed as having premises in Warton Road as well as in Carpenters Road, Stratford. By 1905 the records show that the company name has again changed to the New Lea Valley Distillery Company. However, the distillery appears to have gone out of business sometime between 1905 and 1910 as it is not listed in the Kelly's Stratford Directory for 1908. An Ordnance Survey map for the year 1892/93 clearly shows the distillery buildings being located in Warton and Carpenters Roads with the western end of the site facing the Waterworks River.

We are extremely fortunate to find that in 1887, an Alfred Barnard, who seems to have been a bit of a whisky distillery enthusiast, had written an article for the *Harper's Weekly Gazette*, entitled *The Whisky Distillers of the United Kingdom*. Under the sub-heading *Lea Valley Distillery, Stratford, London*, Alfred gives us a first-hand account of a visit he made to the distillery, probably in the year the article was published. He begins by telling us how he arrived at the distillery from central London by taking a tram-car to Stratford and he then goes on to explain "when the distillery was built, the whole district was a country suburb, and land was very cheap; now with the exception with a few fields at the back of the works, every inch has been built over and almost absorbed in the great City." Alfred further suggests that the Lea Valley Distillery is the only malt distillery in England.

Thought to be the picture of the former 19th-century Lea Valley Distillery

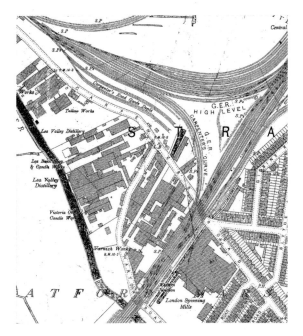

19th-century map showing site of the Lea Valley Whisky Distillery, Stratford

From the article we learn that a guide for the distillery takes Alfred through numerous departments and buildings and explains the purpose of the various machines and storage vessels. During the tour we are told that the distillery produces whisky from both grain and malt, both of which are delivered by barge. The malt travels down the River Lea and the Lee Navigation from Ware in Hertfordshire, arriving at the distillery's Waterworks River docking area. Interestingly, water for the spirit-making process comes from the New River which rises through the chalk from springs close to Ware and is channelled to London via, what is effectively, an artificial canal. This water also receives a re-charge, in dry seasons, from the River Lea via the New Gauge building, located just north of Ware. Water from the upper reaches of the River Lea was considerably cleaner and less polluted than that of the water further downstream which was subjected to industrial waste and effluent discharges as it travelled southward on its journey towards Stratford and the River Thames.

Alfred's enthusiasm and quest for knowledge, has allowed us, in the 21st century, to experience the workings of the Lea Valley distillery in the 19th century. This is a wonderful example of recording an interesting story (that many of us can also do, or perhaps we might wish to chronicle another type of event) so that information, that would otherwise have been lost, can be passed on to inquisitive future generations. As it has often been said, "when it's gone it's gone".

References

Barnard, Alfred, *The Whisky Distillers of the United Kingdom*, *Harper's Weekly Gazette* (1887)

Correspondence and conversations with Richard Durack, at the Newham Local Studies Library & Archives, Stratford, London

Lewis, Jim, *Water and Waste, four hundred years of health improvements in the Lea Valley*, Middlesex University Press, Hendon, London (2009)

VANISHED LIKE A CHILD DEVOURING A SHERBET LEMON – THE LOST INDUSTRY OF CONFECTIONERY

People of a certain age, living within the Lea Valley region and beyond, will no doubt have memories of going to the local sweet shop on a Sunday afternoon to spend a few of their hard-earned "old pennies" on a few ounces of gob-stoppers, or some other confectionery delights, served by a friendly shopkeeper and handed across the counter in a small white paper bag, only to have their purchases stolen on the way home by the older siblings or friends. Those children who lived in Wood Green, Hackney Wick or Forest Gate might have just caught the sweet smell, wafting across the rooftops, from the factories that once provided them with their weekly treats!

Now buried below the International Broadcast Centre on the Queen Elizabeth Olympic Park is the footprint of what was the UK's largest confectionery manufacturer, Clarnico. Founded in 1872 as Clarke, Nicholls & Coombs, the factory in its heyday employed around 1,500 people. Initially its main products were candied peel followed by marmalade, jams and sweets. The company became famous for its mint creams, liquorice and a variety of other favourites winning the taste buds of both young and old.

Clarnico's Hackney Wick factory was ideally placed to receive regular deliveries of sugar and other essentials as it was situated close to the River Lee Navigation. Speedy deliveries of main ingredients like sugar, coupled with the popularity of its products, helped accelerate the company's early growth. By the early 20th century Clarnico had devoted some of its profits to creating social activities for its workforce by forming a brass band and also a hundred-strong choral society. The factory also invested in its own fire and ambulance service.

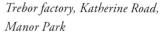

Barratts factory, Wood Green, rock-making department

Trebor factory, Katherine Road, Manor Park

An artist's (over the top) impression of Barratt & Co. Mayes Road, Wood Green c1920s

Barratts caramel and toffee department c1950

During the Second World War the factory sustained considerable bomb damage and this, coupled with the introduction of wartime sugar rationing meant that Clarnico's future looked decidedly bleak. During the post-war period, like several other sections of British industry, Clarnico had failed to modernise its factory and production facilities. In 1969 the company was sold to its confectionery neighbour Trebor, located in Manor Park, East London. This company was founded in 1907 by the partnership of William Woodcock, a sugar boiler, Thomas King, a grocer, Robert Robinson, a grocer and Sydney Marks, a salesman. Each invested £100 to set up a company to manufacture boiled sweets. The name Trebor originates from Robert spelt backwards.

Trebor had not stagnated and had continually updated and invested in improving their manufacturing techniques. By the late 1920s they had introduced powdered sugar into their manufacturing processes which later allowed them to come up with some of their most famous products such as Refreshers and Extra Strong Mints. The post-war period saw Trebor grow and diversify. In 1960 they acquired Jameson's Chocolates; the following year Edward Sharp & Sons of Maidstone was added to the list. By the late 1960s Trebor was Britain's largest confectionery exporter selling to almost 70 countries, with America as the largest destination.

Maynards, best known for their wine gums, was acquired in 1986 for £8.1 million and only three years later, in 1989, Trebor itself was swallowed up by its much larger rival Cadbury for £120 million.

Charles Riley Maynard, with his brother Thomas, began manufacturing sweets in the kitchen of their North London, Stamford Hill home in 1880. Next door, Charles' wife Sarah ran a small sweet shop where she sold the products from the kitchen. In 1896 Charles and Thomas founded the Maynards sweet company. The enterprise became so successful that in 1906 the brothers moved their business into a new factory a short distance away in Vale Road, Wood Green. Situated close to the New River, an historic man-made waterway that brought clean drinking water into the heart of London from springs in Hertfordshire, the factory was able to use the clean water in their production processes.

Just after the turn of the century, Charles Gordon Maynard, son of the founder, suggested that the factory should start manufacturing wine gums. Charles senior, a

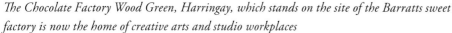

The Chocolate Factory Wood Green, Harringay, which stands on the site of the Barratts sweet factory is now the home of creative arts and studio workplaces

The chimney of the old Maynards factory, Harringay

Methodist teetotaller, was appalled by the idea until his son finally convinced him that no alcoholic infusions would be used in the sweet making process. In 1909 Maynards Wine Gums were introduced to the buying public and by 2002, annual worldwide sales of this popular confectionery brand had reached £40 million. However, the Maynard family did not reap the benefit from these 21st century worldwide sales.

Like many famous company names their individual histories can become consumed in the merger and takeover business, and like fish in the sea, the larger ones swallow the minnows and the even larger ones get swallowed by even larger ones and the brands eventually become lost. In 1990, Maynards was taken over by Bassetts, a Sheffield company, associated with the famous Liquorice Allsorts brand. Therefore, it seems a rather cruel trait of business that the original wine gum maker had lost out to an even larger fish!

Barratt & Company Limited, Manufacturing Confectioners of Wood Green was founded by George Osborne Barratt. George had come from a bookbinding family but decided not to follow the profession and began work as a pastry cook. After marrying Sarah in 1847 he independently set up a sugar confectionery business with the help of his wife and a sugar boiler employee at Shepherdess Walk, Hoxton, London. The business grew rapidly and neighbouring properties were bought to extend the factory.

George came up with a sweet that was cheap and popular with children which he called Stickjaw. The product increased in popularity and it soon became obvious that more factory space was needed. However, by 1880 further expansion at Hoxton was not possible and on his searches across London George found, and was able to purchase, a factory in Mayes Road, Wood Green, which had belonged to the piano manufacturer, Allsopp & Company.

In the early 1880s further buildings were added to the Mayes Road site although in 1889 expansion was slowed by a serious fire in one of the main buildings. The structure was quickly rebuilt. By the late 19th century Barrett's employed 2,000 workers and claimed to be the world's largest sugar confectionery factory in the world.

The old Maynards factory, Tottenham (now Harringay)   *1960s view of Trebor factory, Manor Park*

Over the years, despite economic recessions and two World Wars, the factory continued to expand. By 1955, although the workforce had halved to 1,000 from its earlier peak, presumably due to the introduction of modern machinery, the employees were still able to turn out some 300 tons of confectionery per week. Also, the product lines of sweet varieties manufactured had increased to 200. However, like many of the confectionery companies before them, in 1966, Barratts had succumbed to the creeping takeover obsession and were bought by Bassetts for a reported £4 million.

The death of the Lea Valley confectionery industries was finally confirmed in 1989 when Bassetts were devoured by their larger rival Cadbury-Schweppes for the princely sum of £91 million. Not entirely unexpectedly, in this dog-eat-dog frenzied game that these large multinational companies seem to enjoy, in 2010, after lengthy negotiations, Cadbury was bought by the American giant Kraft Foods who paid £8.40 per share, valuing Cadbury at a staggering **£11.5 billion.**

Interestingly, although the Lea Valley confectionery industries have gone, their ghosts still remain in some of those popular sweet brand names such as Bassetts, Maynards and Trebor.

The old Clarnico factory,
Hackney Wick

References

Author unknown, *A Refreshing Change: Trebor*, Trebor Archive (December 29th 2015)

Ingrams, Sarah, 'Sweet success turns sour for Hackney Wick confectionery company', *Hackney Gazette* (13th August 2012)

Opie, Robert, *Sweet Memories*, Pavilion Books, London (2008)

Plowright, Dennis, *Barratt & Company Limited, Manufacturing Confectioners, Wood Green*, Greater London Industrial Archaeological Society (GLIAS) (2004)

Richardson, Tim, 'Get your hands off our sweets', *The Guardian* (January 16th 2010)

PART TWO

(HISTORICAL FOOD AND DRINK CONNECTIONS THAT REMAIN)

THE LEA VALLEY GROWERS' ASSOCIATION
FOUNDING FATHERS

On Tuesday 31st of October 1911 a meeting of representatives from the Nurserymen and Growers of the Lea Valley was convened at the Imperial Club, Waltham Cross when a resolution was moved by the Chairman and passed by those attending; "That an Association be formed which shall be called 'The Lea Valley and District Nurserymen's and Growers' Association". The passing of a second resolution set the annual membership subscription at ten shillings and six pence (half-a-guinea) that would translate to 52.5 pence in today's money! Unfortunately, the minutes of the meeting do not list all those in attendance so we are unable to compare the numbers of those initially taking up membership of the organisation with the current membership of The Lea Valley Growers' Association (LVGA) as today's organisation has become known.

It is clear from the minutes that the nurserymen and growers were facing a number of quite serious challenges which they had reasonably concluded would only stand a chance of being resolved if they came together as a bona fide organisation. By forming an Association, the growers felt that they would have a better opportunity to solve their problems collectively as certain government agencies would only recognise those organisations that were properly constituted.

The minutes of the first meeting reflect a number of outstanding concerns that the growers would like addressed and, during discussion, the following issues were raised:

(a) The study of the various insect and fungoid pests and diseases which were yearly increasing.

(b) The question of rating which had just been discussed at the meetings of the Cheshunt District Council.

(c) Lectures.

(d) Difficulties with the Railway Companies, Market Salesmen et cetera.

BRITISH GLASSHOUSE PRODUCE MARKETING ASSOCIATION, LIMITED.—MEMBERS OF COMMITTEE.

Top Row Left to Right—A. B. Lister (Sec.). A. R. Wills. J. C. Cobley. C. C. Chorley. C. F. Camburn. G. N. Edwick.
Front Row Left to Right.—C. H. Shoults. G. F. Shoults. J. Harnett (Vice-Chairman). E. S. Shoults (Chairman).
C. J. Randall (Hon. Treasurer). A. A. Pollard. R. Minard.
Absent Members of the Committee.—N. G. Bonaparte-Wyse. A. J. Henriksen. S. Holmberg. A. G. Linfield.
J. Poupart. E. Stevens.

Members of the British Glasshouse Produce Marketing Association Committee, July 1925

While later minutes show that not all the growers' problems could be resolved by coming together as an Association, they do demonstrate that the organisation rapidly grew in stature and was acting in a professional and democratic way on behalf of its members.

By November, after listening to advice from Dr Russell of the agricultural Rothamsted Experimental Station, Harpenden, a special sub-committee of growers was formed. Soon the sub-committee was recommending that members should seriously consider a highly ambitious scheme to set up a local experimental station to carry out scientific work for the organisation. Should the recommendation be approved, then costs for setting up and running the station would be shared partially by funds raised by the growers. The LVGA would also approach the Board of Agriculture and the County Councils of Essex, Hertfordshire and Middlesex for grants to make up the outstanding costs for the station's continued upkeep.

In the following year representation was made by the Council of the LVGA to the Board of Trade over the practice undertaken by some wholesalers and retailers of removing labels from tomatoes, cucumbers and grapes grown abroad so they could be passed off as English produce. Presumably this devious removal of labelling was done so that the perpetrators could command a higher price for their produce. While it would be naive to believe that the Council could win every battle taken up on behalf of its members, the minutes show that the Council representatives went about their duties with a great deal of dedication and energy. They were certainly not afraid to tackle the major service providers over cost increases and there was no hesitation in confronting government departments on issues such as tax and legislation that affected the horticultural industry. The Lea Valley and District Nurserymen's and Growers' Association had begun the task of supporting its members with great enthusiasm; getting this newly formed body off to a flying start.

References

Lewis, Jim, *A Century of Growing the History of the Lea Valley Growers' Association from 1911 to 2011*, Libri Publishing Ltd, London (2011)

Minute books of the Lea Valley Growers' Association 1911-1935

1) Mr. H. O. Larsen, the Popular President.   (2) Mr. J. C. Cobley, one of the founders and the first Secretary.   (3) Mr. A. B. Lister, Live-wire Organizer and Secretary.   (4) Mr. C. H. Shoults, Vice-President and Hon. Treasurer.   (5) Mr. R. Minard, Chairman of Council.   (6) Mr. F. J. Sandberg, a popular member of the Council.   (7) Dr. W. F. Bewley, Director of Experimental Station.

An artist's impression of Lea Valley growers from The Horticultural Trade Journal, 21st November 1923

THE LEA VALLEY GROWERS' ASSOCIATION FACES DELIVERY PROBLEMS AND ENTERS A CRITICAL PERIOD IN ITS HISTORY

The Lea Valley Growers' Association (LVGA) were about to enter a critical phase in their organisation's long history, the period after the Great War. The minute books of the Association highlight just how serious the situation had become.

Throughout the years 1925-1926 there was a continuing stream of correspondence, meetings and visits between the LVGA and representatives of the London & North Eastern Railway Company over ongoing unresolved complaints of late deliveries of produce to the markets around Britain. Also, there were accommodation and storage issues at local Lea Valley railway stations which had yet to be resolved. Ironically, even after all the contact and communication from the LVGA, the growers learned, through press reports (June 1926), that the railway company planned to update the facilities at Cheshunt, Broxbourne and Rye House Stations. As might be imagined the news did not go down well with the growers and the secretary was yet again instructed to write to the railway company. This he did by alluding to the press report and making the point that "we trust this would include all stations in the Lea Valley district".

The seemingly dilatory response by the railway company to the growers' requests for improved local facilities so that produce could be handled more efficiently is difficult to understand. As early as 1879 the Great Eastern Railway Company (later to be grouped into the London & North Eastern Railway in 1923) had opened its own fruit and vegetable market at Burford Road, on the south side of Stratford High Street, East London, which at the time was a state-of-the-art complex. The facilities consisted of two lines of warehouses 220 yards long that were separated by a 40 foot roadway, with railway lines running along the back of each row of buildings so that produce could be loaded directly into storage. Capacity was such that the designers claimed that 200 trucks could be unloaded simultaneously. The long warehouses were divided into separate units and the railway company leased these out to various businesses connected with the wholesale and retail fruit and vegetable trade.

Coal delivered by rail, an essential fuel for the early Lea Valley glasshouse industry

It is known that the LVGA had dealings with the Stratford Market as the Council Minutes of 10th June 1925 allude to, "provision of truck and warehouse accommodation for a certain salesman at Stratford". One would have thought that because the railway company had direct experience of handling perishable products in their own right, they would have responded more speedily to the growers' requests. Perhaps there could be an explanation as it is known that the railway company was dealing with businesses in Hamburg and Holland and in later years an express train would arrive at Stratford in the early hours of the morning bringing produce

from the Continent via the Harwich-Zeebrugge ferry. Because the Continental growers were in competition with their Lea Valley counterparts, and would have been important railway customers, could it be that an 'understanding' had been reached with the railway management?

Looking at the whole railway episode and the continuing niggling wages disputes of the growers, from the position of the 21st century, it is hard to believe that Britain had, compared with today, a relatively strong industrial economy. Therefore, the question has to be asked, were these particular issues a microcosm of a greater set of underlying problems which would lead to our eventual economic difficulties?

The year 1926 was a memorable one not only for the LVGA who agreed, at their October Annual General Meeting to become a Branch of the National Farmers' Union, but also for all of Britain, whose transport system was plunged into chaos when the General Strike began on 4th May. The reasons for the dispute are complex and have their roots in 1924 when the coal owners agreed to increase the wages of the coal miners. In 1925 the government of the day re-adopted the gold standard and set the exchange rate for the pound sterling against the American dollar at the higher pre-war rate, rather than the lower level that it had reached. This resulted in making exports uncompetitive, causing a fall in industrial output. The knock-on effect for employers was to see their profit margins reduced and they therefore demanded a return to lower wages. The Miners Federation refused to accept such terms and the stage was set for the dispute to escalate. However, the miners were at a distinct disadvantage in any future negotiation as there were relatively large stocks of coal available. The miner's leaders appealed to the General Council of the Trade Union Congress and in July 1925 the Railwaymen and the Transport Workers placed an embargo upon the movement of coal.

The General Strike ended in confusion only nine days after it had begun. In his analysis of the dispute, labour historian Henry Pelling blames certain trade union leaders for its collapse as they had failed, in their negotiations, to wring any concessions out of government. Sadly, the effects of the strike are still felt to this day, as resentment remains between small groups of families living within former mining villages. Also, it has left lingering divisions across the mining community. The reasons for these lasting emotions emanate from stories of those mining ancestors who crossed picket lines, the absolute transgression for any trade unionist, being passed down the generations. These feelings were reinforced in recent years by the Miners' strike of 1984-1985.

Of course, the General Strike had caused serious problems for Lea Valley growers. The country still had to be fed and the lack of public transport meant that produce could not be moved to the markets around Britain via the railway network. Fortunately, for the growers, the General Council of the Trades Union Congress had not called out the agricultural or horticultural workers, so produce could still be processed. This meant that private transport could be arranged to get the output of the nurseries to market.

As the transport difficulties caused by the General Strike were fading from the growers' memories, the minutes of the LVGA, November 1926 Council Meeting, revealed a more immediate and serious problem for the Lea Valley horticultural industry to deal with. A grant of £200 for the year 1926/1927 was allocated, with little hesitation, to the Turners Hill Experimental and Research Station to find ways

Food lorry being escorted by armoured car during the General Strike of 1926

of combating an infestation of the red spider mite. The pest was known to be particularly virulent amongst plants grown under glass, extracting the contents of leaf cells which produced a mottling effect on the upper leaf surfaces. If not treated swiftly, the leaf can wither and drop off with the possibility of the plant eventually dying. Future LVGA minutes show that the growers were continually allotting substantial sums of money to the Turners Hill Experimental and Research Station to find a solution to the red spider mite infestations that seemed to occur regularly.

The year 1927 began with members of the LVGA being appointed to serve on three prominent bodies, the National Council of Agriculture, the National Farmers' Union Headquarters' Fruit and Vegetable Committee and the Glasshouse Growers Sub-Committee of the Fruit and Vegetable Sub-Committee. Being invited to serve on national bodies would suggest that the LVGA were recognised by their peers as important players within the horticultural industry.

The possibility of establishing a canning factory in the Lea Valley was raised at the Council Meeting of 12th January by the LVGA's secretary who reminded the members that help for such an enterprise could be given by the Ministry of Agriculture. In fact, the canning factory idea had been raised some years before as it was thought that the establishment of such a plant would have been a successful way of dealing with tomato surpluses, but this early initiative seems to have been shelved. On this later introduction of the scheme, it was proposed by Mr C. H. Shoults, one of the prominent Council members, and unanimously agreed by the meeting, that "under the present conditions the proposition was impracticable".

The statement probably gives us an insight into the tight economic conditions that many businesses across Britain were experiencing at the time. This view is reinforced later in the year when the thirteenth annual dinner, which was to be held in November and attended by the Minister of Agriculture, was cancelled, "owing to the very depressed condition of the industry".

It has been estimated that paying for the First World War had cost Britain 25 per cent of her national wealth. On the horizon, less than two years away, the western industrial world was about to feel the severe economic effects of America's "Wall Street Crash", with the collapse of hundreds of banks and the wiping out of stock market shares prices. This economic meltdown would lead to a period of severe austerity named the "Great Depression" that would remain throughout the 1930s.

The next event of the LVGA's January calendar was a special Extraordinary General Meeting on 27th when it was unanimously agreed that the rather cumbersome title, the Lea Valley and District Nurserymen's and Growers' Association Limited, which had remained attached to the organisation since the inaugural meeting in 1911, should be changed to the more user-friendly Lea Valley Growers' Association Limited. Also, at about this time, the LVGA had received information that plans were afoot to move Covent Garden Market to Bloomsbury. For reasons which are not clear, the LVGA took great exception to the proposition and then did what it usually did in such circumstances; passed a resolution. The proposer was once again Mr C. H. Shoults, who suggested that the following resolution should be sent to the National Farmers' Union, "That this meeting of the Lea Valley Growers considers the proposed removal of Covent Garden Market against the interests of growers and urges the National Farmers' Union to oppose the Bill".

It is impossible to learn, from the minutes, the reasons why the LVGA were so against the Market being relocated and it would be difficult to imagine that the growers had any thoughts of wanting to preserve Covent Garden's rich historical heritage; they probably knew very little about it. Interestingly, the area acquired its name around the 13th century when it was once part of arable land and orchards belonging to Westminster Abbey and referred to at the time as "the garden of the Abbey and Convent". At the dissolution of the monasteries, under King Henry VIII in 1540, the grounds were acquired by the Earls of Bedford and it was the Fourth Earl who commissioned Inigo Jones to build a number of stately houses on the land. By the mid-1600s a small open-air market had set up in the area but it was not until the 1830s that the first neo-classical building was erected to cover the market which, by all accounts, had become a disorganised sprawl. Over the years Covent Garden

The former Stratford Vegetable Market, Burford Road

became Britain's largest and best-known fruit and vegetable market. We now know that the proposal to move Covent Garden Market to Bloomsbury did not take place and that the suggestion was either a rumour or perhaps the LVGA's resolution was successful after all. As post-war congestion grew in the area of central London the authorities quickly realised that the Market's future was limited. Land was acquired at Nine Elms, Vauxhall in the early 1970s and the New Covent Garden Market was built. In 1974 the old Covent Garden Market relocated to the new address.

Over the years the LVGA had regularly complained about the imports of cheap fruit and vegetables, particularly tomatoes, from countries such as Belgium, Holland and Spain and had tried, unsuccessfully, to get successive governments to impose an import produce tax from these countries. Had such an arrangement been implemented, it would have reduced the imports of foreign produce, allowing Lea Valley growers to sell more of their crops to the markets of Britain. Of course, the government would have been well aware of the risks of introducing such a levy on imported fruit and vegetables as the countries concerned could easily impose punitive taxes on British goods entering their respective markets.

However, in spite of all the external economic pressures and the influence of two World Wars, the LVGA, although radically altered in its marketing and horticultural set-up, has remarkably survived these trials and tribulation and is now, at the time of writing, bracing itself for the next major challenge of the UK's Brexit negotiations!

References

Lewis, Jim, *A Century of Growing the History of the Lea Valley Growers' Association from 1911 to 2011*, Libri Publishing Ltd, London (2011)

Minute books and correspondence of the Lea Valley Growers' Association, Turners Hill, Cheshunt, Hertfordshire

FOOD, DRINK, FILMS AND WAR – THE CONTINUING STORY OF THREE MILLS

There is only one place in London where there are tide mills with recognisable structures from the period in which they were built. Newham is indeed fortunate to have two of these mills within its boundaries in the district of Bromley-by-Bow. The four undershot wheel House Mill, built in the late 18th century and the three undershot wheel Clock Mill, built in the early 19th century.

In my earlier books I have been able to explain how the first President of Israel, Dr Chaim Weizmann, came to work at Three Mills during the Great War, a fact that was not generally known. Here, at the former Nicholson's gin distillery within the 19th-century Clock Mill, he perfected a manufacturing process for distilling acetone from grain. This important ingredient was required in the manufacture of cordite, an explosive used in shells, during the Great War. However, there are many other interesting stories attached to this quite extraordinary site that is situated in a conservation area in the lower Lea Valley just north of where the River Lea becomes Bow Creek.

The history of the site, now known as Three Mills at Bromley-by-Bow, goes back a long way. In the Domesday Survey of 1086, it is recorded that in the Manors of East and West Ham there were eight mills, formerly nine. Currently, it is not possible to say with absolute certainty that any of these were situated on the present-day site of Three Mills. However, until further evidence is uncovered, which either confirms or denies this, it might be fair to conclude that one or more of the mills referred to in the Domesday Survey probably did occupy the site. Today only two mills remain from a different period, the House Mill built by the second Daniel Bisson in 1776 and the Clock Mill erected by Philip Metcalfe in 1817. The clock tower, bell and clock face of the latter building are from an earlier mill c1750, as are the two drying kiln towers. Both the House Mill and the Clock Mill were of the tidal type and employed undershot wheels, four in the former and three in the latter. Advantage was taken of the tidal properties of the lower reaches of the River Lea, fed from the River Thames, when the energy from the incoming tide was stored and used to power the mills. The high tide was allowed to flow uninhibited through a central channel below the House Mill and around 57 acres of water (the surface area) was penned in the channels behind the mill to achieve the necessary force to sustain prolonged operation. When the tide began to ebb individual sluice gates could be opened, in a controlled way, behind each water wheel, in both the House and Clock Mills, allowing

Dr Chaim Weizmann (1847-1952), scientist and the first President of the State of Israel

The House Mill and the Clock Mill at Bromley-by-Bow at high tide

Lloyd George who insisted that Dr Weizmann should be rewarded for his work at Three Mills

the returning current to create the power to drive the grinding machinery and to operate the grain hoists. In 1938 it was calculated that, by using this system of stored energy, both mills could operate for periods of between six to eight hours on each tide thereby achieving 12 to 16 hours working a day.

Research carried out by Dr Keith Fairclough and Mr Brian Strong of the River Lea Tidal Mill Trust would suggest that the early mills on the site were in the possession of the Abbey of Stratford Langthorne (founded in 1134-1135 by William de Montfichet), until Dissolution of the Monasteries occurred in 1538 under King Henry VIII.

According to Dr Fairclough, for centuries before 1728 the Three Mills had been an important corn mill supplying raw materials for the Stratford and London bakers. The only exception to this pattern was that during the reign of Elizabeth I part of the facilities were used for brief periods to produce oil or gunpowder and that in the 18th-century part of the facilities were used in the preparation of cloth.

As has already been suggested, there are many interesting stories that can be written on the subject of Three Mills, but the one that I should like to feature here is about what might be termed an 18th-century environmentally friendly food production system that was both efficient and profitable.

When Peter Lefevre, the son of a Huguenot immigrant, purchased Three Mills and leased the nearby St Thomas Mills in 1728 the future activities of the site was about to change dramatically. Lefevre, who was a baker and a meal-man, had wanted to continue flour production at the mills. However, in less than a decade, Lefevre and his partners had decided to diversify their interests by setting up a brewing, distilling and pig breeding business. Dr Fairclough has used the insurance records of the Lefevre business and the companies that followed, between the mid-18th and early 19th centuries, to estimate the size of the operation, which he concluded "was extremely large". In making this deduction, Dr Fairclough had taken insurance information that had been used to calculate the premiums paid on a known design of Arkwright's Derbyshire cotton mill and compared this to the amount paid by Lefevre.

Nicholson's Copper still in Three Mill Studio restaurant

Nicholson's gin distillery, Clerkenwell

Three Mills industries of brewing, distilling and pig breeding appear to have formed a highly successful integrated production system that took place on a site of around 15 acres. The milling process produced flour for the bakeries of London and also prepared grain for the production of malt, beer and alcohol. Waste material from these processes was fed to pigs that would eventually become bacon. Curing had the advantage of giving the bacon a much longer shelf life than uncured meat, which meant it could be sold in relatively small quantities. In the days before refrigeration, bacon could provide a good source of protein to supplement the diet of the less well off, particularly those who were drawn to London to seek work and had to live in overcrowded and unhealthy conditions.

The replacement Helping Hands memorial on Three Mills Green

The former Nicholson's distillery, now Three Mills Film Studios

In their business partnership, Peter Lefevre and his nephew John would appear to have maintained their enterprise on a sound commercial footing through obtaining contracts to supply large quantities of bacon to the Royal Navy. Their business at Three Mills also had the advantage of allowing transport costs to the Navy storehouses to be kept to a minimum. The Royal Navy Victualling Yards were at Deptford, a short distance up the Thames from the mouth of the River Lea so it would have been quite a simple matter to move the product by water.

Lefevre was one of the larger London distillers and this side of his business was also profitable. Much of the raw alcohol produced at Three Mills was sold on to other distillers in the capital for the production of gin and other spirits. In the early part of the 18th century gin was a popular drink among the working classes and with Lefevre's brewing capacity he had the ability to satisfy both the beer and spirit markets.

Although tide mills operating on the lower reaches of a river appear to be a good and sensible idea there can be a number of drawbacks for other users of the river such as millers, landowners and barge masters. For example, the artificial maintenance of water levels by penning can cause considerable problems for conventional millers (those simply using the flow of the river to obtain power) in the near vicinity by slowing the natural flow or quickening and increasing the reverse flow of the tide. Also, on a number of occasions, those with tide mills who had control of the water would deliberately allow the levels to get above the recommended heights that were permitted by the river authorities. This caused flooding of the surrounding areas, which made life difficult for the smallholders and livestock keepers who were trying to scrape a meagre living from the low-lying land. And of course, the artificial changes to the height of the water in the navigable river and corresponding channels caused many difficulties for the barge masters who were often delayed and had to suffer the financial consequences. Such were the conditions in which our industrial ancestors, who depended on the river and the surrounding land for their livelihoods, lived and worked.

When Daniel Bisson had the present House Mill erected in 1776, he also constructed a new house, as living quarters, on its eastern side. For its day the project was a major undertaking with four waterwheels driving eight pairs of grindstones (these were increased to twelve pairs in the 19th century). Remarkably the House Mill remained in operation until 1941, when, due to grain shortages and enemy action during the Second World War, it was forced to close.

Three Mills at Bromley-by-Bow with the tide out

Memorial erected c2001 that stands 150 metres north of the site of an earlier memorial cross on Three Mills Green. This memorial was vandalised and later replaced.

Interestingly, the Clock Mill, which was built by Philip Metcalfe (1733-1818) in 1817, has survived with a quite different history. Metcalfe, who seems to have had a varied business career, which included a spell in the wine trade, had also, by 1784, become an MP in the government of William Pitt the younger. According to Dr Keith Fairclough, who has carried out much research on the subject, Metcalfe acquired Three Mills in 1759 when he bought out the Huguenot partners John and Peter Lefevre. Following this acquisition, he set up a new partnership, which only lasted a few years, but included his son Daniel and two other family members. In 1763 a new 14-year partnership was established, with a capital of £46,000, to carry out business as 'Miller Malt Distillers in the Rectifying way and dealers in Brandy and Rum and in corn'. The partners were Daniel Bisson the elder (£22,000), Daniel Bisson the younger (£15,000), Philip Metcalfe (£6,000) and Roger Metcalfe (£3,000). In 1780, Metcalfe had gained control of Three Mills. He then took the decision to turn the management of the business over to his nephew.

By the age of 47 Metcalfe had become a very wealthy man and on leaving his house at Three Mills he took up residence in Savile Street (now Row), Westminster where he began to live the life of a gentleman of means. Four years later he purchased his seat in parliament and represented the constituency of Horsham in Sussex, becoming a staunch supporter of the Prime Minister, William Pitt the younger. During his political career he spent considerable sums of money to purchase other parliamentary seats, although some of these ventures into maintaining a parliamentary presence were unsuccessful.

After Metcalfe's death, on 28th August 1818, his nephews James and Henry ran the business. By 1872 the business was heavily in debt and bankruptcy occurred. J. & W. Nicholson, who, in the early 19th century, had established a gin distillery in St John Street, Clerkenwell, London offered a little over £60,000 for the business. This was accepted.

The name gin is said to be a corruption of the French genievre or the Dutch junever, both meaning "juniper". This alcoholic beverage, distilled from grain and flavoured with juniper berries, had become a cheap and popular drink in 18th-century Britain, particularly among London's poor. Hogarth, in his engraving *Gin Lane*, depicts the social deprivation brought about by the drink. Here he shows the dwellings of the poor as slums and those of the pawnbrokers and moneylenders as grand. The popular saying "Drunk for a penny, dead drunk for two pence" would appear to describe the evils of imbibing to excess.

When Nicholson's took over at Three Mills considerable sums of money were spent in making improvements and also in the construction of new buildings. It would also seem that their marketing was to a different class of customer than to the poor and their product was different. Nicholson's produced a dry gin, unlike the earlier gins that were sweet and enjoyed by the working class. In fact, one of Nicholson's advertisements claimed that "Gentlemen of refined and educated palates would take no other, and no butler would dare to introduce any other brand at the Clubs …"

As mentioned earlier, during the Great War (1914-1918) the distillery buildings were used to carry out experimental work to see if acetone, a solvent used in the making of cordite (a smokeless explosive), could be distilled in bulk to support the war effort. Doctor Chaim Weizmann had developed the process and, during this time, he worked at Three Mills to see the project through. Weizmann's work is referred to by Lloyd George in his memoirs and the following passage is quite revealing:

> When our difficulties were solved through Dr Weizmann's genius, I said to him: 'You have rendered great service to the State and I should like to ask the Prime Minister to recommend you to His Majesty for some honour'. He said: 'There is nothing for myself'. 'But is there nothing that we can do as recognition of your valuable assistance to the country?' I asked. He replied: 'Yes, I would like something done for my people'. He then explained his aspirations as to the repatriation of the Jews to the sacred land they had made famous. That was the font and origin of the famous declaration about the National Home for Jews in Palestine.

We now know that the above passage refers to the setting up of the State of Israel, to which Dr Weizmann was elected President in 1948.

By 1952 milling and distilling had stopped at the Clock Mill and a little later most of the plant and machinery was removed. The buildings were then turned over to bonded warehousing, storage and a bottling plant. However, after a dispute with Islington Council over water usage in 1966, Nicholson's took the decision to transfer their gin production facility from Clerkenwell to the Three Mills site. The transfer of plant and equipment took four months to complete. To celebrate the move an official ceremony was arranged for the 15th June 1967 and the chairman of the company, Mr W. R. Nicholson, gave an opening address. Here he proudly announced that "We have been making Gin as a family for five generations and we hope to go on a great deal longer."

Alas, the chairman's hopes for the future were not realised and after a later amalgamation with a major brewer the Nicholson family vacated the site.

By the late 1980s the state and preservation of the 18th-century House Mill was causing the local authority concern. Under a consortium of private and public sector partners, led by the Lee Valley Regional Park Authority, the first work to restore the building began. Later, in the 1990s, more restoration work took place with the support of English Heritage and the Stratford Development Partnership. A further programme of development followed this, when European funding was secured to rebuild the miller's house as a Visitor and Education Centre. Here school groups come to learn about the history of the region and also to participate in environmental projects. The House Mill and the Miller's house are now under the management of the River Lea Tidal Mill Trust.

The Clock Mill, like the House Mill had also endured a period of neglect. However, in the mid-1990s the Workspace Group PLC, a company dedicated to providing affordable accommodation to small and medium-sized enterprises (SMEs), acquired the House Mill and its associated buildings. A visionary plan for the site was drawn up and the buildings have now been given a new lease of life in the form of Three Mills Film Studios. Now the Clock Mill and the other former industrial buildings are used to make films for the cinema and television. It would therefore seem that the 'spirit' of Three Mills is set to live on at Bromley-by-Bow!

Winston Spencer Churchill (1874-1965). During the First World War, when First Lord of the Admiralty, Churchill asked Chaim Weizmann if he could manufacture 30,000 tons of acetone

Three Mills film studio entrance

Three Mills, Bromley-by-Bow, a good place to start to discover the Lower Lea Valley

Visiting the site of Three Mills today, now designated a conservation area, there is an immediate feeling of being transported back in time to a period when the working day, for many, consisted mostly of manual labour. It should not be too difficult for the visitor to imagine noisy wagons rumbling past, heavily laden with sacks of grain that were on their way to the mills for grinding. Visions of grain hoists lifting sacks from a line of parked wagons to the upper floors of the mills with the characteristic rattle of chain on metal pulley are there if we care to be immersed in the ancient atmosphere of this time-locked place. We can imagine wagons leaving the mills loaded with sacks of freshly ground flour, the faces of the drivers smudged white. Accompanying this frenetic activity are the shouts and whistles of the wagon drivers controlling their horses; the smell and snorting of these majestic animals as they pass, straining at the harnesses; the sound of their metal shod hooves slipping and scraping as they try to maintain grip on the slippery cobbled roadway. Some of the wagons leave trails of grain from leaking sacks. This will provide a welcome meal for the watching pigeons perched high on the surrounding buildings. The rodents that live on the banks of the nearby River Lea will consume those grains that are missed when they emerge to feed after dark.

What is so remarkable about the site of Three Mills is that there has been ongoing milling in the area for around one thousand years. Apart from the references in the Domesday survey, research has shown that, in Elizabethan times, the mills that then occupied the site were used briefly for the processing of oil and also gunpowder. It was not unusual to convert mills to this latter activity in time of war when the demand by the army and navy for explosives dramatically increased. Early in the 18th century the mills were being used to prepare cloth. However, the main activity of the mills, over the longer and more stable periods, was the grinding of grain to produce flour for the bakers of London.

Our early ancestors, who made the decision to locate their milling complex on the tidal section of the lower River Lea, would appear to have been blessed with considerable planning foresight. Not only did the waterway provide power to turn the mills but it also allowed bulk quantities of grain to be brought right up to the site for easy unloading. And of course, the river provided a plentiful supply of water for the brewing and distilling processes. How many industries today can claim to have planned such an environmentally friendly infrastructure for their business?

With such a long and interesting history the author would like to suggest that schools and colleges bring their students to Three Mills and allow them to soak up the atmosphere of the place. Learning in such a unique environment can be great fun.

References

Author unknown, *Stratford's Hidden Heritage*, Lee Valley Regional Park Authority (1995)

Author unknown, 'Nicholson's Switch Gin Making to Three Mills Distillery', *The Wine & Spirit Trade Review* (23rd June 1967)

Fairclough, Keith, *The Three Mills Distillery in the Georgian Era*, River Lea Tidal Mill Trust Ltd

Fairclough, Keith, *Philip Metcalfe (1733-1818) The MP and Industrialist who Built the Clock Mill*, River Lea Tidal Mill Trust Ltd

Fairclough, Keith, *Owners of the Three Mills (1539-1728)*, River Lea Tidal Mill Trust Ltd

Fairclough, Keith, *The Lefevre Family and Distilling Along the Lower Lea*, River Lea Tidal Mill Trust Ltd

Fairclough, Keith & Strong, Brian, *The Bisson Family of Three Mills*, River Lea Tidal Mill Trust Ltd

Gardiner, E. M., *The Three Mills Bromley by Bow*, Wind and Watermill Section of the Society for the Protection of Ancient Buildings, London (1957)

Lewis, Jim, *London's Lea Valley Britain's Best Kept Secret*, Phillimore & Co. Ltd, Chichester (1999)

Lloyd George, David, *War Memoirs, Vol. 2*, Odhams Press Ltd, Watford (1933)

Pick, Christopher, *Changing Environments; London Working Spaces Past and Present*, Workspace Group PLC, London (2000)

Strong, Brian, interview (1st November 2002)

Weizmann, Chaim, *Trial and Error the Autobiography of Chaim Weizmann*, Hamish Hamilton, London (1949)

Appendix

A memorial of 2001, which became vandalised, once stood about 150 metres north of the site of an earlier memorial cross on Three Mills Green, part of the Lee Valley Regional Park Authority. Carved into the stonework of the memorial were the following words:

> Of your charity pray for the souls of Thomas Pickett, Godfrey Maule Nicholson, Frederick Elliott and Robert Underhill who lost their lives in a well beneath this spot on 12th July 1901. The first named in the execution of his duty was overcome by foul air; the three latter descending in heroic efforts to save their comrades shared the same death. Godfrey Maule Nicholson rests in Privett churchyard, Hants and the other three were laid in Wood Grange Park Cemetery.

A new memorial was erect, just south of the site, to replace the one that became vandalised.

Note. To discover what's on at the House Mill at Three Mills, Bromley-by-Bow go to website (http://www.housemill.org.uk/whats-on/). Further information can be obtained by telephoning: 020 8980 4626.

THE POLITICS OF FOOD – THE NEW SPITALFIELDS MARKET AND THE CONTINUING EUROPEAN DEBATE

In his 15th annual speech to the National Farmers' Union in January, 1960, the President, Lord Netherthorpe (6th January 1908 – 8th November 1980), (formerly Sir James Turner), warned members of his extreme anxiety when he said, "… we must continue to keep the most careful watch on agricultural development in Europe. I must confess that I am extremely anxious about a Europe divided between 'Six and the Seven'. Agriculturally, we are at the receiving end. If for example, under their new common agricultural policy, which involves the use of the complete apparatus of price support and import control, the Six expand their production, there will be nothing to stop the surplus from arriving on our market". The "Six" which Lord Netherthorpe referred to were the European States of Belgium, France, Italy, Luxembourg, Netherlands and West Germany who, on 25th March, 1957 signed the Treaty of Rome, that came into effect on 1st January 1958 and established the European Common Market, which we now know as the European Union.

What had clearly concerned Lord Netherthorpe was that Belgium and the Netherlands, two of Lea Valley growers' biggest horticultural overseas threats, were among those early members of the European Union. Netherthorpe was convinced that the Six were apt to expand their production over the next few years and would most likely be looking for "export outlets outside the Community".

In concluding his speech, Netherthorpe had some sound advice for the long-term survival of Britain's agricultural and horticultural industries when he made four very knowledgeable, and telling, points.

New Covent Garden Market, Nine Elms, Battersea

First, he expressed the view that:

> In Europe we must work for a European agricultural agreement between the Six and the Seven. If we do not achieve this, we are likely to be the main sufferers from the diversion of agricultural trade emerging from the economic division of Europe.

Second, he made the point that:

> Our role on the domestic front is to produce from our limited acres as efficiently as we are able by applying technical improvements, and by the most economic use of resources to reduce our unit costs of production. To this end the availability of adequate capital, properly used as a tool of good management is vitally necessary.

The third piece of advice was:

> … we must also adapt our production, as to quantity, type, quality and consistency, to meet the challenge of developing and changing consumer demands. The prospects of achieving this on a sufficiently broad scale are bedevilled by the fact that our industry is composed of a multiplicity of small and thereby weak, individual enterprises. Collective effort, the only source of greater strength, and its growth, is conditional upon real cohesion, involving as it does either some willing sacrifice of unfettered independence or agreement to statutory enforcement through agricultural marketing legislation.

And last but not least Netherthorpe made a rather telling observation when he said:

> Failure to co-operate means inevitably the clash of interests and the encroachment on each-other's field of endeavour. Vertical integration in itself [is] no solution even though in other countries it may have proved a threatening menace. Forward thinking in joint endeavour offers more fruitful prospects.

It is interesting to note how visionary Netherthorpe was in his outlook and his analysis of his beloved industry. Here he had identified areas of concern such as the European Union, technical improvements, changing consumer demand and the need for co-operation that posed threats and challenges for the future British agricultural and horticultural industries.

For many years, along with the National Farmers' Union, the LVGA had been lobbying government to have an extra duty levied on foreign tomatoes arriving in Britain. On May 5th 1960, much to the relief of the Association, the government announced that two pence would be levied on each pound of imported tomatoes during "certain periods of the season". However, in the budget the following year, it was announced that there would be an extra two pence duty per gallon levied on fuel oil. Naturally the growers were up in arms over the increase as it was argued they had been encouraged by government to switch away from solid fuels to make economies and to change to oil as an alternative means of heating their glasshouses. The reader will no doubt recognise that when governments try and balance the books it is normally inevitable that there will be winners and losers or, in some cases, stagnation.

When making his speech at the LVGA's 37th annual dinner in November 1962, held at the Savoy Hotel, Lieutenant Colonel Leach, Chairman of the Executive Committee, expressed his reservations about Britain's entry into the European Common Market when he said, "Now, the negotiations for British entry to the Common Market give rise to problems for British horticulture unparalleled in our history. As you well know, I have strong reservations on the matter both on broad constitutional and commonwealth grounds". In his reply, on behalf of the guests, Harold Woolley, President of the National Farmers' Union, referred to the Union's stand, "which is very firm, regarding the Common Market" and made the following revealing statement "If for reasons outside our responsibility, they exonerate themselves from the pledges that they have given. We shall do all we can to see the Common Market arrangements recognise horticulture's position, and that the government does not ride off on the excuse that circumstances have changed". These types of feelings were widely held at the time and the topic of the Common Market and the European Union still evokes considerable emotion today (2019) as evidenced by the acrimonious and divisive Brexit debate.

The Old Spitalfields Market at the beginning of the 20th century

In an article entitled *Growers Must Face Greater Demand for Standardisation*, in the December 1962 News Letter, Eric Gardiner, Chairman of the National Farmers' Union Central Horticultural Committee, made some extremely far-sighted observations when he wrote, "We have seen come into being chain stores and supermarkets, which have moved into the realm of fruit and vegetable selling, even in a few isolated instances into flower selling. It seems almost certain that this method of selling will develop appreciably and ultimately we may well see some forty to fifty per cent of our fruits and vegetables sold in this way, though nothing like that for flowers". He then went on to say "This must lead to a greater demand for the standardised product – a greater demand for the product that can be bought on sample". The LVGA will no doubt recognise how right Eric Gardiner was.

At the 1965 Annual General Meeting of the National Farmers' Union two interesting resolutions were moved by representatives of the LVGA. These resolutions open a window on the membership's concerns regarding the future of the horticultural industry. In the first it was proposed that "This Annual General Meeting, whilst welcoming the move of Covent Garden Market to a new site south of the Thames, urges the National Farmers' Union to investigate the possibilities of setting up a market in the North London area". Here we see that the Lea Valley Growers' are losing their traditional market and they now want a replacement facility that is nearer to their nurseries.

Construction of the New Covent Garden Market began on a 57 acre site at Nine Elms, Battersea in 1971 and the market officially opened for trade in 1974. In 1991 the old Spitalfields Market was relocated to a 31 acre site at Leyton, in the London Borough of Waltham Forest. The market is now referred to as the New Spitalfields Market. Originally located just outside the City of London, the market can trace its origins back to 1638. It was Charles I who gave a licence for "flesh, fowl and roots" to be sold, on what was then, Spittle Fields. The site in Leyton now borders the northern end of the 2012 Queen Elizabeth Olympic Park.

The second resolution was quite different and is centred on the question of tariffs, but on this occasion, ironically ones that were imposed on British produce. "This Annual General Meeting deprecates the import regulations operated by other countries, including the Commonwealth, which makes it difficult for British growers to export their produce, and urges either greater facilities be afforded to the Home Industry or the British Government should impose similar restrictions on imports to the United Kingdom." This is a classic example of the consequences of placing tariffs on imports. Retaliation by the overseas countries is normally sure to follow and the restrictions imposed may not be directed just towards horticultural products.

References

Lewis, Jim, *A Century of Growing the History of the Lea Valley Growers' Association from 1911 to 2011*, Libri Publishing Ltd, London (2011)

Minute books and correspondence of the Lea Valley Growers' Association, Turners Hill, Cheshunt, Hertfordshire

Correspondence and private conversation with Lee Styles, Secretary of the Lea Valley Growers' Association, (February 2019)

FLOUR POWER IN THE LEA VALLEY

Over the years, in my earlier books, I have been privileged to follow the history of an extraordinary Lea Valley miller who continues to expand and innovate his business by keeping up with current technology and also maintains a loyal and hardworking workforce.

In 1867 George Reynolds Wright came to Enfield and entered into partnership with James Dilly Young the miller of Ponders End Mill, taking up residence in the East Mill House. The house, built in the reign of Queen Anne, is in active use today providing the necessary accommodation to administer the only independent family run flour mill in London. Speaking to directors and staff of this company will immediately reveal a love and enthusiasm for a proud tradition of milling at Ponders End, whose roots can be traced back as far as Domesday.

By the early years of the 17th century the mill was known as Flanders Mill. Power to drive the seven pairs of millstones came from the River Lea via two breast water wheels. Evidence of this earlier water power can still be observed today. If a visitor stands on the bridge, which is part of the Lea Valley Road running between the King George and William Girling reservoirs, and looks north, a weir will be seen which allows water from the river to enter the mill head stream that passes directly below them. In the 18th century the mill became known as Enfield Mill, changing its name again halfway through the 19th century to Ponders End Mill.

In the early days of milling, flour had to be delivered to the bakeries of London and the surrounding area by horse-drawn wagon. A typical day for the carman would start around 6am when he would leave the mill with a full load of five tons, ensuring the route he took did not have too many steep and difficult slopes. After a round trip of some ten to twenty miles he would return about 7pm, not finishing the day until his main asset, the horses, had been fed, watered and stabled. Next day, an appointed operative would come to work early in the morning to see that the horses were harnessed and ready for the day's deliveries.

CEO David Wright in a moment of thoughtfulness!

A small sample of Wright's product range

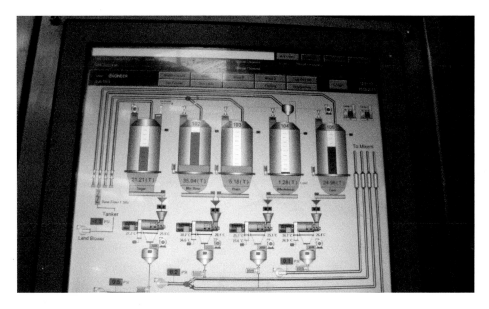

Computer monitoring of the production processes at Wright's new facilities

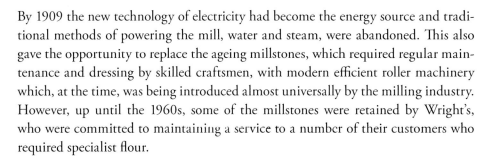

George Reynolds Wright (1824-1914) founder of Wright's Mill at Ponders End

By 1909 the new technology of electricity had become the energy source and traditional methods of powering the mill, water and steam, were abandoned. This also gave the opportunity to replace the ageing millstones, which required regular maintenance and dressing by skilled craftsmen, with modern efficient roller machinery which, at the time, was being introduced almost universally by the milling industry. However, up until the 1960s, some of the millstones were retained by Wright's, who were committed to maintaining a service to a number of their customers who required specialist flour.

The early 20th century also brought with it an improved road network and in August 1906 the company took advantage of this by acquiring a steam wagon. This new technology dramatically increased the amount of flour which could be transported compared with the horse-drawn wagon. However, steam wagons of the day

Modern packing and labelling machinery. Where are the workers?

had certain drawbacks. Initially these vehicles had solid iron wheels which caused considerable problems for their drivers when descending or ascending hills with bulk loads of between 15 to 20 tons, particularly when the roads were icy or wet.

Those were hard times for our ancestors, but we can be proud of their achievements which have helped successive generations of Wrights to invest confidently in the future of the mill, preserving part of the Lea Valley's rich industrial heritage.

The year 1938 brought a significant leap forward in the fortunes of the mill when the directors, no doubt with expansion firmly in mind, purchased, from the Metropolitan Water Board, freehold ownership of a little over 11 acres of surrounding land and the entitlement of passage for barges from and to the Lee Navigation.

When the Second World War commenced in 1939 the mill came under government control. To help secure food supplies for the nation, and to supplement the losses caused by the bombing of the mills situated in the London Docks, the production at Ponders End was considerably increased. This was achieved by extending the working of the mill to seven days a week and 52 weeks a year for the duration of the war. Fortunately, the mill did not suffer any serious damage from enemy action although the constant operation of the plant had taken its toll on the machinery.

By the early 1950s, with the mill back in family control, the decision was taken to modernise and refurbish the plant and machinery. The specialist firm of Thomas Robinson of Rochdale was called in and by April that year, only ten weeks after modernisation began, the mill recommenced production with a 50 per cent increase in capacity. Flour could now be processed at the rate of 12 280lb sacks per hour.

Company expansion still continues beyond the millennium with improvements in buildings and equipment and the introduction of silos for bulk storage of grain and flour along with a new nearby storage facility. Modern methods of production call for changes to the way in which flour is transported, so Wright's have invested in bulk road tankers. No doubt the 19th century wagon driver would have found these new methods of storage and delivery impossible to imagine.

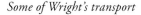

Some of Wright's transport

The late Ian Pearce, BBC Three Counties Radio, taking time out to photograph while recording a story with the author at Wright's Mill. In the background is the famous Deb the Bread

The miller's house, Wright's Mill

Not resting on their laurels, the directors of Wright's have responded to changing public tastes, by introducing a number of new product lines particularly aimed at today's busy consumer. Speciality flours and bread mixes, which can be made quickly and easily, now appear on many supermarket shelves and expansion into overseas markets is an ongoing feature of the business strategy.

The author, in his former industrial role, has worked with businesses within eastern and western Europe and from the Middle to the Far East and has never come across an operation quite like Wright's Mill. The Mill has successfully incorporated a range of buildings, some listed, that date from the 16th century into an efficient modern-day manufacturing facility.

Anyone visiting Wright's Mill in the 21st century could not fail to become immersed in an atmosphere of energy and also be impressed by the forward thinking of the

The old mill pond and head stream to Wright's Mill

management as the company looked for new and challenging business opportunities. This "can do" spirit led to the decision to greatly expand and modernise the production facilities, a step not taken lightly as there were considerable long-term cost implications. Once the decision was taken, things moved quickly. In the year 2000 new warehouses were built and Buhler's, the Swiss Milling Engineers, were commissioned to install state-of-the-art high-speed packaging and palletising equipment. When the then English Cricket Captain, Nasser Hussain, opened the newly built units in November 2001, they were acclaimed as the most sophisticated packaging and storage facilities in Europe.

The Ponders End site now consists of a blend of ancient and modern buildings. However, the casual visitor could be forgiven for thinking that the facilities and processes behind some of the more elderly facades matched their quaint exteriors, but these assumptions would be totally wrong. For example, once inside the old mill itself it is perfectly possible to imagine that you have somehow been transported into another dimension and have accidentally stepped across the threshold of Doctor Who's time travelling machine, Tardis. For inside is a multitude of sparkling modern milling machinery that allows the Mill to comply with the exacting regulatory standards and procedures of ISO 9000 and also the stringent Hazard Analysis Critical Control Points (HACCPs).

Investment in an on-site laboratory and bakery has allowed sampling and testing to be carried out at each stage of production and every delivery of wheat arriving at the Mill is also sampled by an automatic probe and the results recorded. Not satisfied with the high level of quality control that has been put in place, Wright's management wished to investigate the environmental impact of their manufacturing processes. To this end they commissioned an independent audit of their operations and the resulting recommendations have been implemented.

It is clear that the heavy investment in plant and machinery and also the detailed attention to product quality is already paying off as export opportunities have opened up to the West Indies, France, Bulgaria, Belgium and beyond. This has resulted in the company being recognised when the Managing Director, David Wright received the prestigious crystal trophy presented by the organisers of the Trade and Investments' Passport to Export programme. This was followed, in 2004, when Wright's Flour won the Manufacturer of the Year at the London Business Awards.

In January 2013 the building of a new factory was begun at Delta Park, Enfield, a short distance from the Ponders End mill, and like many of Wright's well-managed projects the plant opened for business in January the following year. Here, in this new facility speciality products are stored, mixed, bagged and processed. Also, within the building an innovative bakery has been installed where new products can be developed and tested. This facility also allows Wright's to provide important technical support for their valuable client base.

After celebrating their 150th anniversary in 2017, Wright's again looked towards the future. Since building the new factory at Delta Park, David Wright had been on the lookout for a suitable site, within the Lea Valley region, to build a further factory as demand for his products has increased year on year. Unfortunately, perhaps due to the Lea Valley's popularity as an expanding food and drink hub, no suitable land was available. Naturally, David was disappointed, as he wanted to keep his

Women workers on the pre-pack line at Wright's Mill c1948

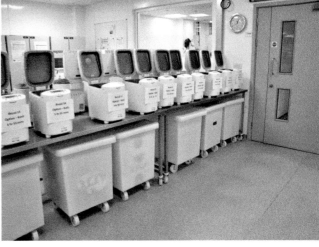

Wright's laboratory where all different brands of domestic bread making machines are product tested

businesses close together in an effort to protect the environment by keeping food miles travelled by his transport fleet to a minimum. After scouring the countryside adjacent to the Lea Valley David was able to find and secure a suitable site only ten miles away at Harlow in Essex where a new factory is currently (2018) under construction.

Many companies might feel that once they had invested considerable sums in new plant and machinery, they could relax for a time but not Wright's, as the programme of investment and the developing of new products continues apace. David Wright is the fifth generation of the family involved with milling at Ponders End since his ancestor George entered the business in the 1860s. Fortunately a sixth generation of Wrights, James, after graduating from the world-renowned Swiss Milling School in St Gallen in 2013 and gaining experience through working in different departments of the mill, has been appointed Production Director. This is refreshing to observe as many young people today do not opt to follow in their parent's footsteps.

Over the years many Lea Valley companies have come and gone, but Wright's Mill stands as a glowing example of determination and entrepreneurship, a symbol of the ability of a family business to adapt product and processes to the needs of a highly competitive and ever- changing industrial world. The example of progression from Wright's early Lea Valley roots and the company's successful expansion into the 21st century must surely act, not only as encouragement to other firms wishing to set up in the region, but as a continuing reminder of how to adapt and prosper. Here are important lessons for us all to learn and perhaps the Wright model, or should we say the "right model", can supply some valuable clues for industry in general, pointing the way to future regeneration within the region.

References

G. R. Wright & Sons Limited, *The Story of a Family Business*, (undated brochure)

Wright, David (current Chairman of G. R. Wright & Sons Ltd), interview (August 2018)

Authors unknown, *Wright's, 150 Years of Milling, Celebrating 150 Years Through Pictures and Cuttings*, self-published (2017)

FROM BARROW-BOY TO FOOD TYCOON – A LEGEND IN HIS LIFETIME

Jacob Cohen was born in Whitechapel in London's East End, into a poor immigrant family from Poland, on 29th October 1898. His father, Avroam, a harsh disciplinarian by all accounts, had lived with his wife and family in abject poverty while working as a tailor in the sweatshops of London. By long hours and sacrifice he was able to move his family to 26, Darnley Road, Hackney where he established himself as a jobbing tailor, doing sub-contract work for manufacturers in the garment trade.

Young Jacob, who had begun school at the age of six, left education when he was only 14 and like many children of his generation he received school reports which carried the not untypical remarks, "must try harder" and "lacks application". With the young man's career prospects looking decidedly bleak, on leaving school he first began work for his brother-in-law, Morris Israel, in the street markets of London. After a short spell in the market he joined his father's tailoring business and worked long hours into the night making buttonholes in jackets, for which he received only pocket money. Jacob hated the long hours and the strict regime of his father's business and looked for an opportunity to escape.

In March 1917, at the age of 18, the opportunity to escape the drudgery of the rag-trade came when he enlisted in the Royal Flying Corps (RFC) as an air mechanic. After completing his basic training, during which he suffered racial abuse, he reluctantly allowed himself to be known as Jack rather than Jacob to avoid making his ethnic origins too obvious. His first posting was to Roehampton where he worked as a rigger on barrage balloons before being sent to the Middle East. While entering Alexandria harbour his troopship was torpedoed by an enemy submarine and Jack, a non-swimmer, was almost drowned. Luckily, he survived this ordeal and the rest of his war was relatively uneventful. He was demobilised from the RFC in 1919.

A young Jack Cohen after becoming Air Mechanic second-class (number 64535)

Jack's sign being installed at first UK store 19th September 2018

Map of Tesco Campus, Welwyn Garden City

Jack's reward for war service, along with many of his contemporaries, was unemployment, a fate that certainly did not suit his character. Although his father had asked him on a number of occasions to re-join his tailoring business, Jack did not relish the thought of losing his hard-won independence. With limited skills to offer, Jack's mind drifted back to the time when he had worked for his brother-in-law in London's street markets. Now, with a demobilisation gratuity of £30, Jack hired a barrow and invested the rest in a quantity of ex-NAAFI (Navy, Army and Air Force Institutes) foodstuffs which were probably surplus to requirements after the cessation of hostilities. Now pushing his recently purchased barrow to Well Street, Hackney, in London's East End, Jack was fortunate in being able to rent part of a site from a market trader where he was able to sell his NAAFI purchases. In his first day of trading he sold £4 worth of groceries, of which 25 per cent (£1) was profit. Soon Jack mastered the 'show business' ways of the market traders, selling tinned milk, *not at three-pence, not at two-pence – it's yours for a penny*. Broken biscuits, golden syrup, tinned jam et cetera, were all disposed of in a similar way to his working-class customers who were always on the lookout for a bargain. In the harsh reality of East End life, low prices were a key to Jack's growing success. Within six months of starting his business, Jack was trading in at least two other East End markets.

Tesco CEO David Lewis at Jack's opening in Cambridgeshire 19th September 2018

Tesco tea 1924

Therefore, it would appear that Jack had found his real niche in life and, as his biographer has pointed out, he had become not only a tradesman but also an entertainer.

The next few years were quite eventful for Jack. He moved his stock out of his father's house, which had virtually become a warehouse, and took a small lock-up in Clarence Road, Clapton, East London to store his ever-increasing amount of goods, until larger premises were found in the Upper Clapton Road. By 1920 an account was opened with the Midland Bank in Hackney, a sensible move, as the takings from one of his stalls in the Caledonian Market had exceeded £100 in a single day. In only two years Jack was operating from around six London markets and he had also established himself as a supplier of groceries to other traders. In January 1924 Jack married Sarah (Cissie) Fox and her £500 dowry, along with £130 in wedding gifts, was wisely placed in a Post Office savings account. A house was rented in Gore Road, Hackney and it was there that their two children were born, Irene in 1926 and Shirley in 1930.

In late 1924, although he did not realise it at the time, Jack Cohen was about to take on new business that would prove to be a lasting tribute to his entrepreneurial skills. During his buying and selling forays in the food trade Jack had met T. E. Stockwell, a

The Snowball Building Tesco Welwyn Campus

Well Street Market, Hackney where Jack Cohen began selling NAAFI surplus goods after the First World War

partner in the tea-importing business of Torring and Stockwell. Jack arranged to buy tea from the company in bulk at nine pence (3.7p) a pound and to sell it on in half-pound packs at six pence (2.5p) each, a mark-up of 25 per cent. A brand name for the tea was established by combining the initials of his supplier, T. E. Stockwell, with the first two letters of Cohen making the now famous name of the food giant TESCO.

Jack Cohen died in 1979 after creating a retail empire that would change the shopping habits of the buying public forever. The name TESCO lives on as a fitting epitaph to this entrepreneurial man, not just in Britain but internationally. However, it is doubtful that the majority of customers who flock daily through the doors of the company's supermarkets around the world, could remotely guess how the name TESCO came about.

In the four decades since Jack's death TESCO expanded at a pace, overtaking Sainsbury's by the mid-1990s as the UK's largest food retailer. 2000 saw the launch of Tesco.com and the supermarket continued to expand its range of clothes, electrical and personal finance products. In 2009 a joint venture with the Royal Bank of Scotland saw the establishment of Tesco Bank and the following year its first zero-carbon supermarket was opened in Cambridgeshire. However, at about this time, the subprime mortgage crisis in the United States of America was beginning to cause ripples in the financial markets around the world and Britain was in no position to escape its grip. This had a serious effect on household disposable incomes as banks rushed to tighten their lending arrangements. The knock-on effect saw families changing their grocery buying habits by visiting the low-end food retailers and of course this caused TESCO and the other established UK supermarkets to rethink their purchasing and expansion strategies.

It has taken a little time for the world financial markets to settle down and allow TESCO and the other UK supermarkets to improve their profitability. At the time of writing TESCO reported a group operating profit in the year to the end of February 2018 of £1.28 billion. However, the current TESCO CEO, David Lewis, and his management team cannot rest on their laurels as many market problems loom ahead, with uncertainties over Britain's trading relationship with the European Union and, the current reduced purchasing power of a weak pound affecting the cost of buying food, fuel and other goods from abroad. Also, there is the added problem of the relatively new German owned supermarket chains taking a large share of the UKs food and drink market. To combat this threat, in September 2018, TESCO launched their new cut-price store in Cambridgeshire under the name Jack's. The name is to commemorate the founder of TESCO, Jacob (Jack) Cohen.

Perhaps when next crossing the threshold of your local TESCO supermarket, particularly in 2019, the company's centenary year, don't forget the name and legacy of Jacob Cohen who founded his grocery empire with a demobilisation gratuity of £30 in 1919.

References

Archer, Fiona, Interview at Tesco Head Office, (February 2000)

Lewis, Jim, *London's Lea Valley, More Secrets Revealed*, Phillimore (2001)

Personal communication between the author and the Tesco Press Office and the office of the Tesco CEO

Powell, David, *Counter Revolution, the Tesco Story*, Grafton Books, London (1991)

Wood, Zoe, 'Low prices, no frills: can Tesco's secret plan defeat Aldi and Lidl?' *The Observer* (16th September 2018)

H. FORMAN & SON – LAST MAN STANDING!

Ask the average Londoner where he or she thinks the "creators and purveyors of the world's finest smoked salmon" are based and you will probably be met with a blank stare. The answer, of course, is Stour Road, Fish Island, Hackney Wick, London E3 2NT. This is the address of the new collection of H. Forman & Son businesses; comprising of smoke house and head office, Forman's London restaurant, Forman's Smokehouse Gallery and the Forman's Fish Island venue. Boris Johnson, the former Mayor of London, officially opened the completed smokehouse, designed by Jones East 8 architects, in 2009. The building, in pink, resembles the shape of a darne of salmon (a portion cut through the whole salmon fillet) and looks spectacular, particularly when lit up at night and viewed from the east side of the Lee Navigation towpath. However, the journey of Forman's to the site within 100 metres of the 2012 Olympic stadium was anything but straightforward.

At the beginning of the 20th century, Harry (Aaron) Forman left his home in Odessa, Russia and arrived in London's East End to begin a new life. Like many Jewish immigrants before and after him, Harry brought few possessions with him apart from his skills as a fish curer. Initially, in about 1905, he started his business in Stepney by importing Baltic salmon in barrels of brine but soon realised that there was already a plentiful source of the fish much closer to home. At the time Scottish salmon was arriving at London's Billingsgate Fish Market so Harry was now able to acquire fresh produce locally that had not been brine soaked in barrels for months. Before refrigeration this was one of the many techniques used to preserve fish, an important food source that is difficult to keep fresh.

After a short time of trading and experimenting, Harry went on to develop a delicately flavoured smoked salmon which became very popular, particularly with his Jewish customers. The oak smoking process that he had created became what is now known as "the London Cure". Here the fish is subjected to a dry-curing process using only salt followed by a cold-smoking procedure that is created from the friction-burning of oak logs. This process remains a feature of H. Forman & Son smoked salmon business to this day allowing them to claim to be "creators and purveyors of the world's finest smoked salmon". The product was recently awarded, in 2017, special Protected Geographic Indication (PGI) status which places it alongside other gourmet food and drink like Parma ham and champagne.

A darne of salmon

Forman's suffer fire damage at former Queens Yard site   *Forman's suffer flooding at former Queens Yard site*

When Harry's young son Louis was growing up, he was often taken by his father on buying trips to Billingsgate Market and he also visited other establishments in the London fish trade. According to Lance Forman, currently the owner of H. Forman & Son and great grandson of Harry, it was such trips that provoked Louis to ask a stream of questions about the fish trade that caused Harry to seriously think and consider his present business status, causing him to establish the salmon smoke-house business of H. Forman & Son. Reading Lance's enjoyable book, *The Forman's Games, the Dark Underside of the London Olympics*, it is clear that Harry and Louis bounced ideas off each other and became a formidable business team as by the late 1920s the company was thriving. Like all businesses that have become successful many have learned the hard way that success can be short lived and it is always necessary to continually seek new markets. Clearly Harry and Louis had learned this lesson early on in their careers and they both set about taking their smoked salmon brand upmarket. High-end stores and restaurants were approached and new contracts with customers like Selfridges, Fortnum & Mason, the Ivy and Mirabelle were secured giving Forman's a necessary boost in status.

Louis took over the business from his father Harry and later relocated to an address in Ridley Road, Dalston where he ran the company up to the 1960s. On the death of Louis, the business passed to his son-in-law Marcel Forman who in the early 1970s moved the company to a purpose-built building in Queens Yard, off White Post Lane, Hackney Wick.

At the time of the move there were growing external pressures from the expanding supermarket industry who were demanding lower prices from the smoked salmon producers and Marcel point-blankly refused to succumb to their demands. For him Forman's had never cut corners and had always traded on quality and this policy of maintaining taste and texture was not going to change on his watch. He probably had not realised at the time that his stubborn stance would, in the future, see the Forman name become the last man standing amongst the smoked salmon producers. All the other East End salmon smokers would eventually go to the wall as they reduced their product quality and profit margins in an effort to satisfy the savage demands placed on their industry by the large food retailers.

Marcel was keen to ensure that the Forman name continued and when his young son Lance was looking forward to his school holidays, instead of long summers

H. Forman & Son restaurant,
Fish Island Hackney Wick

of messing around with his mates, his father would take him to the factory for a 4am start so that the lad could begin the process of learning the business from the bottom up. Lance would also be taken on his father's business trips to Billingsgate Fish Market and sent out with a delivery driver to get a hands-on feel for the customer base. During these teenage times working in the factory and visiting the markets Lance's hair and clothes became imbued with the smell of fish and it would seem that Marcel may have put his son off from becoming the fourth generation of Forman's to run the business!

After graduating from Cambridge University, Lance did not join the family business but spent the next ten years of his early working life as an accountant, a political adviser and also as a real estate negotiator in Eastern Europe. The skills that he had learned while working in these areas would be put to practical use in the future. However, at the time, Lance could not have known how close the future really was. Meanwhile, Marcel, who had been working a 60-plus hour week, was having thoughts of retirement and responsibility for the day-to-day running of the business had been given to Forman's General Manager.

While Lance was away from the family business, he had always harboured thoughts of one day making a positive contribution and continuing great grandfather Harry's legacy. On learning of his father's retirement ambitions he was shocked to discover how the company had developed over the years, with no proper management structures, employees relying on memory with prices and customer requirements locked in their heads and without a computer programme in sight. Things were made even worse when Lance spoke to the General Manager who told him that the business was doomed as it was unable to compete with the mass-produced Scottish salmon industry that had installed modern plant and equipment and was producing a commodity product.

H. Forman & Son, HQ,
Hackney Wick

When Marcel finally retired, the family business was split equally four ways between Lance and his three sisters. Knowing that it is seldom possible to run a successful business if too many family members are involved, as emotion can sometimes overrule hard-headed commercial decision-taking, Lance negotiated an amicable arrangement to buy out his sisters' shares. On Monday 9th May 1994 Lance became CEO of H. Forman & Son, Salmon Smokers and a new era of business opportunity was about to open up for the company. However, Lance could never have appreciated the obstacles that lay ahead when he took on his new role.

As might be expected the new CEO was quick out of the blocks and for the first time Forman's saw the introduction of a computer system that replaced the need for employees to carry product prices and other details in their heads. Some of the old technology, like the ancient telephone answering machine, was not immediately scrapped. Lance had sensibly realised that the trusted face-to-face relationships that his father had built up and nurtured over the years with his loyal high-end restaurant chefs had to be maintained. It was usual for these people to phone in their last-minute orders and be confident of a next-day delivery as they finished their late-night shifts at around two in the morning and they had become familiar with using the ancient device.

The next major task that Lance faced was to overhaul product marketing, an area ignored by his father who believe it to be a total waste of money. A local design and print firm, Quadrographics, was commissioned and, with Lance's input, completely redesigned the presentation of packaging, introduced a new company logo and created an annual Forman's wall calendar that promoted the gastronomic image of smoked salmon. These calendars, sent to chefs in up-market restaurants, soon found pride of place on their kitchen walls. Perhaps remembering some of the successful ways of his father's hands-on approach to business, Lance began regular meetings with the buyers at leading retailers like Harrods, Harvey Nichols, Selfridges and Fortnum & Mason and arrangements were made to have in-store tastings and other promotional events that considerably raised the Forman's quality profile with affluent consumers.

Lance Forman showing Muhammed Ali that smoked salmon packs a punch!

While these new initiatives were getting increased recognition for the company name, more needed to be done to improve profitability without diminishing, in any way shape or form, the long-held demands for product quality behind the family name Forman. This characteristic of the business had been stubbornly maintained, without compromise, for over nine decades in the face of growing market competition and fortunately Lance had realised that it was the single most important thing that would allow Forman's to stand alone from the competition. Unflinchingly preserving product quality under the Forman's name was the strategy that Lance thought would keep the business moving forward, the temptation to lower prices in the hope of increasing turnover he believed would convey the wrong message to the consumer.

The hard work that Lance had put in was now beginning to pay off and astonishingly, by 1996, the company had doubled in size and the H. Forman name was gaining wider- recognition amongst the taste-conscious public. Lance would be the first to admit that in business you cannot always plan for success, sometimes it comes out of luck, fortunate market conditions and a generous helping of good old-fashioned gut instinct. These attributes all came together in the runup to one Christmas when Forman's flexibility gave them the opportunity to quickly step in and set up the mail order company of Forman & Field allowing them to seize a large slice of the lucrative Christmas hamper market. The initiative created a direct link with the consumer and by creating the "fictitious" Mr Field, Lance had skilfully managed to limit future complaints from his established long-standing customers.

As I have suggested earlier, *"when you believe your business is most successful that is when your business is most vulnerable"* and the following is a typical example of the mantra.

In 1998, the Queens Yard factory, which Lance had previously expanded to cater for his growing order-book, suffered a major fire that took out 60 per cent of the building. While this would have proved disastrous for most businesses it created a backs-to-the-wall wartime spirit of dogged determinism for Lance and his staff.

Louis Forman, son of founder in the Homburg hat with largest salmon caught in 20th century, in 1935

It will be recalled that the company relied on its antiquated answering machine for taking next-day guaranteed delivery orders and it was this extremely important device that was trapped inside the smouldering shell of the factory. Fortunately, John Cherrie, Lance's trusted General Manager, and a fireman were allowed briefly into the building and retrieved the precious piece of kit which, although grime-covered, still worked. Loyal staff who had arrived on site at the start of the fire had acted quickly and removed all the stock from the cold room and transferred it to a refrigerated van. It is probably fair to say that it was these two specific actions that miraculously allowed Forman's to dispatch their orders that day. Clearing a day's orders was one thing but how do you continue supplying your valued customers without a factory and the facilities to cure salmon? Lance was very much aware that if he could not maintain a continuous supply of smoked salmon to his regular customers they would find other sources and this would probably mean that their business would be lost for ever.

Lance had luckily kept his insurance premiums up to date and he was also fortunate in being contacted by a really professional loss adjuster, Nick Balcombe, who immediately took over the logistics of keeping the business afloat. A nearby haddock smoke house was approached and the owners generously offered the use of their kilns while the rebuilding of the Queens Yard factory took place. Six months later Lance and his staff were back in their refurbished premises which had been completely modernised and opened up with a viewing area to show off their salmon processing skills. It is hard to imagine how Lance had coped over the previous six months when covered sides of salmon were manually pushed on trollies across Queens Yard to the haddock smoke house for curing, often under the watchful eyes of health inspectors. No doubt a loyal and trusted workforce had something to do with it. While all this was going on Lance had become a travelling salesman talking up the quality of Forman's salmon to new and established customers and also keeping the conditions that his company was currently working under securely under wraps so as not to alarm his clientele.

In October 2000, just when the business was beginning to prosper in its recently rebuilt premises, tragedy struck again when, after an incessant downpour lasting many hours, the nearby River Lee Navigation breached its banks and the factory flooded to a depth of three feet, completely contaminating the building and all the salmon produce. Despite all the efforts of Lance and his staff to keep the water at bay they were completely overwhelmed as water breached every orifice in the building, even creating a surge in the toilets. Here, we are reminded again of the mantra, "*when you believe that your business is most successful, that is when your business is most vulnerable*".

When the rain and the waters finally subsided a local industrial cleaning company was engaged to supply the necessary equipment and chemicals to dry out the building and to contain the contamination. Now Forman's could at least get back in business, with the agreement of the Environmental Health Officers, albeit on a temporary basis, until a better solution could be found. Unfortunately, the contaminated water had leached into the wall cavities making these parts of the building almost impossible to treat and, as it will be appreciated, this could not be tolerated in the interests of hygiene and food safety. Once again, Lance's trusted Mr Fixit, Nick Balcombe, was called in and tasked with finding a solution that would be permanent. Considering all the contamination problems and the need to keep all Forman's regular customers happy with the delivery service that they had grown used to, there was only one real solution; a new-premises was required.

Fortunately, Nick had been able to negotiate an amicable settlement with the insurers and all the other interested parties and this allowed Lance to sprint out of the blocks and quickly purchase a building in Marshgate Lane, Stratford that had just come onto the market. The deal was completed in 2002 after some legal setbacks, and probably with a great sigh of relief from Lance. However, unbeknown to him at the time, the relocation of Forman's would place their new premises at the centre of a much-needed piece of real-estate regarding the forthcoming 2012 Olympics, an event that was never thought to be coming to East London. Who said that lightning never strikes in the same place as it would seem that the "business mantra" quoted above was about to come back to haunt Lance once more!

Before we continue the Forman story it would seem like a good place to pause for a moment to reproduce a chapter entitled *The Queen Elizabeth Olympic Park*, from the author's 2017 book, *From Ice Age to Wetlands the Lea Valley's Return to Nature*. It is now realised, since speaking with Lance, that there is another Olympic Park story about sacrifice that has not received adequate coverage.

On the 6th July 2005 in Singapore, the International Olympic Committee announced that London had won the bid to host the Olympic and Paralympic Games in the year 2012. As the result was announced television crews began interviewing weary, yet ecstatic British officials, who up until then had spent every available moment putting the finishing touches to their bid presentation. Not all, it would seem, had believed that London could pull off this nail-biting win against what many pundits claimed to be the favoured city, Paris. When the television cameras cut to the waiting crowds at Stratford, in London's East End, watchers could not fail to be moved by the scenes of sheer excitement as local residents came to realise that the Games' major facilities would be located on their doorstep in the lower Lea Valley, an area that over the years had seen more than its fair share of industrial dereliction and neglect. For decades, the region had been crying out for a regeneration stimulus of this magnitude and it would seem that the dreams of local people were about to be realised.

The construction of the Queen Elizabeth Olympic Park to accommodate the 2012 Games turned out to be a magnificent opportunity to regenerate not only Stratford, but also the surrounding East End community. This area of east London had remained, for many years, neglected and unloved. As Britain's industrial base, along with the Thames Docklands region, had been in serious decline since the 1970s there was not a faint glimmer of hope that things would change economically for the better in the foreseeable future. It is probably fair to say that the region had never fully recovered from the effects of the Blitz and the unimaginative architectural developments such as the high-rise blocks of flats that had been erected in the 1960s. These high-rise buildings had been constructed with little thought for the well-being of their residents and had isolated members of once tight-knit communities that had grown together and supported each other during the war years.

Perhaps the vision for the current, and ongoing, transformation of Stratford and its East End neighbours can best be summed up by the following statement from the London Legacy Development Corporation:

the ultimate goal is that the Queen Elizabeth Olympic Park becomes a natural extension of its environment, and the boundaries between the Park and its neighbouring communities no longer exist.

Once decontamination of the highly polluted Olympic site and the removal of the electricity pylons had taken place, architects, planners and developers then had the momentous task of creating a 21st century landscape around a tangle of railway lines, waterways and Bazalgette's Victorian sewerage system, all of which crisscrossed the Park like a badly knitted pullover made from spaghetti. Those who had grown up and lived in the Stratford area for most of their lives could not have failed to have been overwhelmed and astounded by the complete transformation of a once

Smoked salmon hanging outside the entrance to the old H. Forman & Sons Factory in Ridley Road

neglected and derelict landscape, that had supported scrap-yards, old and smelly industries like bone renders, varnish works, oil refiners, paint manufacturers and sulphuric acid distillers, in such a relatively short time. In the words of the authors of *The Making of the Queen Elizabeth Olympic Park*, the project came in "… on time, within budget, to multiple stakeholders' satisfaction, and to challenging targets for sustainability, the Olympic Delivery Authority (ODA) established a new benchmark for development everywhere".

In establishing this "new benchmark for development everywhere", the ODA had to displace some 270 businesses which included H. Forman & Son on their new site in Marshgate Lane. Now Lance was about to face the biggest challenge of his life. Since taking charge of Forman's he had successfully managed the business through fire and flood and now he would have to take on the might of state-sponsored bureaucracies and others that had placed a compulsory purchase order on his recently refurbished building. How, in the face of such pressure, that would eventually see off 269 other businesses, could he stand alone and continue the legacy of a successful family firm that had been producing a world-class product for over a century? To answer this question, I would invite the reader to read Lance's personal account in which he graphically describes, in his enjoyable book, *Forman's Games the Dark Underside of the London Olympics*. However, suffice it to say, after a long drawn out battle, Lance's business was really the last man standing on the proposed Olympic Park site.

Eventually, the Olympic authority agreed to a deal with Lance and paid to build a new smoke house, complete with restaurant, art gallery and party venue, beautifully positioned on Fish Island, Hackney Wick and overlooking the Olympic site. After investing heavily in H. Forman and Sons, the Olympic authority actually adopted the Fish Island site as venue of choice for corporate entertainment.

What a joy it is to be able to write a story with such a positive outcome that clearly illustrates how sheer hard graft and determination can win through in the end. Since the 2012 Olympics, Lance's business has gone from strength to strength. Forman's can now boast producing an exceptionally wide range of fish related products including their unique London Cure. These products are being shipped to countries around the world where consumers are now enjoying the tastes and flavours of delicacies from London's East End. On this good news note Lance will not need to be reminded about my mantra; *"when you believe that your business is most successful, that is when your business is most vulnerable"*!

Note

When speaking with Lance Forman the author was surprised to hear a story about the late Jack Cohen, the founder of Tesco, which had never shown up when researching the history of this company. This particular story had come down through the family to Lance and had obviously made a lasting impression on him, so much so, that he wrote about it in his recent book, *The Forman's Games, the Dark Underside of the London Olympics*. I shall reproduce the section here for a little light entertainment!

> My grandfather found that he had a knack of sourcing the best quality fish at the best price and introducing it to the most prestigious customers before any of the rival smokehouses had woken to the opportunity. But, despite the Forman's skill and acumen, they did make an error of such monstrous proportions that has haunted the family down the decades. My grandfather was friendly with an East End barrow boy who was one of life's inveterate hawkers and hasslers, constantly blagging a few coins from shoppers at the local market for some piece of junk he had found lying in the gutter a few hours before. In his teens, the barrow boy decided he wanted to expand, and my grandfather offered him five pounds to finance his growth. Tragically, the deal was structured as loan finance rather than an equity injection. The barrow boy was Jack Cohen, who set up his stall in Well Street Market in 1919 and whose business became known as Tesco. If Harry had been entitled to say, 50 per cent of the share capital, you could be reading a different type of book right now.

As mentioned earlier this story was news to the author, and despite further research, no evidence has yet been found to prove or disprove the family legend. Could it be, what a Jewish friend of the author has termed, "bubamusar", a tale that my grand-mother told?

References

Forman, Lance, *Forman's Games the Dark Underside of the London Olympics*, Biteback Publishing Ltd, London (2016)

Forman, Lance, interview (September 2018)

Lewis, Jim, *From Ice Age to Wetlands, the Lea Valley's Return to Nature*, Redshank Books, Oxfordshire (2017)

MCMULLEN OF HERTFORD – A FAMILIAR NAME IN THE UK'S BREWING INDUSTRY

In around 1790, William McMullen left his native Ireland and settled in Hertford where he ran a nursery business in St Andrew Street. He married Sarah Odwell and the couple had ten children, two daughters and eight sons. The fourth son, Peter McMullen, who became a cooper by trade, founded McMullen's brewery in 1827 which began life in a modest way in Railway Street, Hertford. At the time Peter did not own any public houses, as the company does today, so apart from brewing his beer he also had the added task of having to sell it.

By 1832, the beers had become so popular that the brewery had to relocate to larger premises in Mill Bridge, Hertford and by 1836 Peter had managed to raise sufficient funds to buy his first public house, the Greyhound, located just south of the town of Hertford in the village of Bengeo.

Later expansion of the brewery, to seemingly quench the thirst of the local ale drinkers, saw McMullen move once again in 1891, this time to a newly erected brewery in Hartham Lane. It has been suggested that McMullen's policy of continued expansion, coupled with the decision to only use whole leaf hops, instead of pellets or oils relied on by others that has given the distinctive taste to their ales and beers. This has made their beverages popular with their regular customers and contributed to the success of the brewery.

In 1984, with demand for their beers still rising, the McMullen family took the decision to have a modern brewery built. This new brewery had the capacity to produce 100,000 barrels per year. However, the continuing story of success had a sting in its tail that could not have been foreseen by the family at the time. This would lead to the company teetering on the brink of collapse by the turn of the millennium as by 2002 a split had occurred between the controlling family share-holders. After 175 years of progress, with the company now valued at £176 million, a dispute arose over family members who wished to receive a higher dividend, and those who wanted to reinvest the annual profit back into the company coffers and take a lower dividend. Eventually a reasonable compromise was reached with the chairman David McMullen stepping down and the appointment of Charles Brims who took over the post as an independent chair. Eventually Charles was able to put together a strategy that was acceptable to both sides of the divided McMullen shareholders whereby certain non-licenced property investments were sold and an

Early print of the old McMullen Brewery complex

Peter McMullen, the founding father of McMullen's Brewery

The McMullen Brewery flag

The old McMullen Brewery in Hertford

innovative plan was put forward to mothball the large brewery, with adjacent land being sold to a supermarket. This would help to re-capitalise the company. Also, the plan included the building of a much smaller highly-efficient brewery that would be designed to supply the 130-plus McMullen freehold public houses in London and across the Home Counties.

In 2006 the new Whole Hop House Brewery opened, designed by McMullen's Head Brewer, Chris Evans. While the brewery can only produce 15,500 barrels per year this lower capacity allows the brewery to take advantage of a government scheme, the Progressive Beer Duty (PBD), that permits smaller breweries to pay less tax on their beer. Incidentally, there is a clue in the name "Whole Hop House Brewery", as no doubt the beer-drinking aficionado's will be pleased to learn that the new brewery still brews with whole leaf hops and only uses natural ingredients in all its different beer varieties. Talking of which, the Cuffley Industrial History Society wrote the following in an online newsletter:

> Although McMullen beers are produced from old recipes, AK Original Bitter has a history that is shrouded in mystery and probably pre-dates the founding of the company. It is not known what the initials AK stand for and there are no records of their identity. A few years ago, a campaign was launched by older AK drinkers in McMullen pubs in an attempt to solve the mystery, but to no avail. There were theories galore including the belief that AK stands for Ale Keeper, the brewery worker who, in the 19th century and the early 20th century, acted as a night watchman and kept an eye on the fermenting beers.

However, further research by Fergus McMullen, Production and Sales Director, suggest that the initials AK possibly refer to, "the habit of branding casks with letters to denote style and strength in *Victorian times*". This would seem to be the

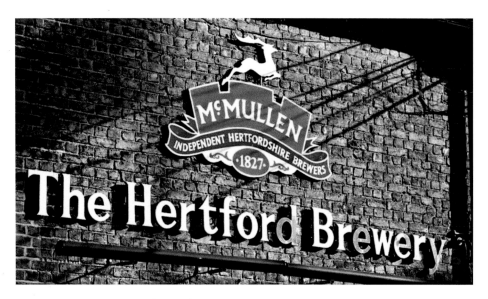

The McMullen Hertford Brewery sign proudly showing their independence

most plausible suggestion that the author has heard to date, but it would be nice to discover archival or other conclusive evidence to confirm or deny the assumption. However, solid evidence might be difficult to come by, as the AK recipe for the beer is thought to be one of the oldest in Britain.

The restructuring of the company in the early part of the century has allowed the independent regional family business of McMullen to continue brewing beer in Hertfordshire for over 190 years, much to the delight of the local community.

References

Author unknown, *McMullen's Brewery*, online newsletter of Cuffley Industrial History Society

Halstead, Tony, 'McMullen's Brewery Saved by Restructure', *The Morning Advertiser* (4th June 2003)

Protz, Roger, *McMullen of Hertford – Change and Survival*, British Guild of Beer Writers (September 2006)

WALTHAM FOREST COLLEGE SCHOOL OF CATERING AND HOSPITALITY

Waltham Forest College has an interesting and varied history. Established in 1938 at Forest Road, Walthamstow as the South West Essex Technical College and School of Art it was one of four regional technical colleges in Essex. Initially, the college was expected to provide education for 1000 full-time day students and 4000 evening students. At the official opening ceremony on 28th February, 1939, Dr H. Lowery, the first Principal, in his address to the gathered dignitaries, summed up the ethos of the College thus:

> We want to make it the people's university. The alternative to academic secondary education that we are going to offer here is the sort of thing for which education-alists have been crying out for years. We are not just providing for examinations. We want to give people a sound knowledgeable background and training on all sorts of subjects. We want to feel that this is their place, a great community centre.

It would appear that Dr Lowery's words have never been forgotten as, on a recent visit to the college, the author witnessed students being taught the necessary skills that employers require to keep our businesses, factories and service industries going.

A certificate awarded to Peter Lewis (WFC) for catering at the Queen's visit to Waltham Forest in 2002

Art students in front of the former South West Essex College c1950

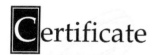

WALTHAM FOREST COLLEGE

Certificate

has been awarded to

Peter Lewis

in recognition of his participation in preparing and serving food at the 'Celebration of Youth and Fashion' event for the visit by Her Majesty Queen Elizabeth II to the London Borough of Waltham Forest on 9 May 2002

Head of School

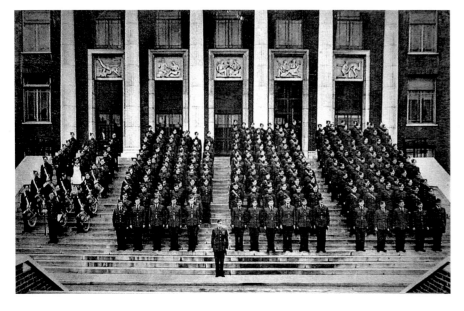

Members of the Royal Air Force on the College steps. These men received technical training at the College during the Second World War

Front entrance to Waltham Forest College, Forest Road, Walthamstow, London E17 4JB

During the Second War the college provided courses for military personnel from the Army, Navy and the Royal Air Force, training them in various engineering subjects. These courses were taught alongside the traditional range of technical subjects that were necessary during time of war. At the time, it should be remembered that Walthamstow and the surrounding region was highly industrialised, and many of the factories and workshops were contributing to the war effort, so trained personnel were in high demand.

In 1965, control of the college passed from Essex County Council to the London Borough of Waltham Forest and the following year the name of the establishment changed to the Waltham Forest Technical College and School of Art.

In the early 1990s, when London's wholesale Smithfield meat market closed its butchery college, Waltham Forest College was invited to replace the facility and took the opportunity to set up a butchery school, The Smithfield Unit, with a teaching staff of three full-time lecturers. The school soon became a popular training establishment for the next generation of butchers and is now recognised by many

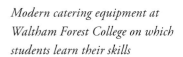

Modern catering equipment at Waltham Forest College on which students learn their skills

food retailers and hoteliers as the place to go to for fully qualified staff. When the school was first established, they would present, each year, the Mayor of London with a decorated boar's head for the Mayor's banquet. Also, students from the Smithfield Unit would carry a large Paper Mache version of the dressed boar's head when taking part in the Lord Mayor's parade. However, in later years these traditions have regrettably been discontinued.

In 2002, the year of the Queen's Golden Jubilee, Her Majesty and Prince Philip visited Waltham Forest as part of the celebrations. As on such occasions a feast is usually prepared to impress the royal

Queen's visit to Waltham Forest, Jubilee year May 2002

Students from the Women's Department 1948

visitors, this was entrusted to the students and staff of the catering and hospitality department at Waltham Forest College. The meal was designed, ingredients sourced and the food prepared, then delivered to Waltham Forest Town Hall. As certificates were awarded to the college staff who took part in organising the catering, it is fair to assume that no complaints from the Royals were received!

On a recent visit (April 2019) the author was taken on a conducted tour of Waltham Forest College hospitality and catering facilities by Dawn Bennett, the head of department and her colleague, Tom Barden. Here the modern kitchen facilities were viewed where students learn their culinary skills under the watchful eyes of experienced chefs, kitted out in dazzling white starched hats and full chef's attire. The facilities for learning were highly impressive, with the latest technology being employed to a degree that would have made earlier graduates extremely envious. Recently a group of students, with their tutors, spent four weeks in Spain learning new cooking skills and also spent time learning the language.

In the latest constructed kitchen ceiling-mounted cameras have been installed which allow students to record and, later, review their skills, while induction hobs give students the opportunity to learn how to cook with the latest kitchen equipment. The kitchens are fitted with adjustable workbenches, allowing full access for students in wheelchairs.

Students at work in Waltham Forest Cookery School 2019

Modern kitchens at Waltham Forest College where expense has not been spared on state-of-the-art equipment

The Waltham Forest College student canteen 2019

The author was allowed time to speak with the students and it was a pleasure to learn about their backgrounds and ambitions for the future. After the tour an invitation to take lunch in the Mallinson restaurant, which is open to the public, could not be refused as sampling a range of delicious foods prepared by the students turned out to be an excellent way of carrying out a very pleasant independent taste test! The result of which was a credit to the students and their teaching staff. The Mallinson restaurant also allows the students to practice their table-waiting skills in a real-time environment that includes the learning of important communication skills that will be necessary in future employment. I am sure that many of us have experienced what should have been a pleasant restaurant meal in a warm inviting atmosphere, spoiled by the attitude of a stroppy waiter who had got out of the wrong side of bed that morning, probably wishing he/she had never chosen the profession!

The staff of the hospitality and catering department have given careful consideration to student needs with a full range of daytime and evening courses that take account of the diverse range of cuisines that are now being offered to the public in a plethora of eateries. The college trains chefs, waiting staff, butchers, bakers, baristas and front of house restaurant staff. There is also a wide choice of apprenticeships offered so that students can learn while they earn.

It is probably not surprising that graduates from the hospitality and catering courses end up being employed by many famous restaurants and hotels, include Waterside Inn, Delaware North, the Ritz and Claridge's.

The author cut his engineering teeth in the now vanished evening class technical college system, where emphasis was placed on teaching students the skills required by local industry. This cannot be achieved without the teaching fraternity of colleges, like Waltham Forest, engaging with target industries within their localities to learn their specific needs and requirements. It was reassuring to discover that this particular model of teaching was being revived by Waltham Forest College. While Britain's industrial base is all but gone, replaced by service industries, which incidentally include hospitality and catering, it is therefore refreshing to see that Waltham Forest College has risen to the challenge of training generations of our young people, creating employment and ensuring that Britain's service industries, that form the backbone of our leisure and tourism market, remain prosperous and competitive.

Waltham Forest College under construction in 1937

References

Bray, W. R., *The Country Should be Grateful*, South West Essex Technical College (1947)

'Essex Education Committee, Education in Essex 1928-1935', Report of the Essex Education Committee (1935)

Discussions and correspondence with Dawn Bennett, the Head of Hospitality and Catering, and her colleague, Tom Barden, Graphic Designer and Marketing Officer

Guided tour of Waltham Forest College hospitality, catering and engineering departments (April 2019)

Lewis, Peter (former supervisor and buyer for Waltham Forest College Catering and Hospitality Department), interview (January 2019)

Reaney, P. H., *The History of Walthamstow*, London Borough of Waltham Forest (1979)

Note

Smithfield (Smooth field), London's wholesale meat market can trace its history back to around the 12th century. The area was once open land where cattle, sheep and pigs could graze and drink, probably in the River Fleet, before being traded and slaughtered.

FROM MILK TO METHANE – THE CONTINUING DEVELOPMENT OF CATTLEGATE FARM, ENFIELD

In all my years of researching and writing about London's Lea Valley region, I never appreciated that the area had so many diverse and interesting businesses all clustered together in one place. The next story that is about to unfold represents one of these remarkable enterprises.

The story begins at the time of the Great Depression of the 1920s when Britain was just beginning to economically recover from the effects of World War One. In 1925 the government restored the pound sterling to the "gold standard" at the pre-war exchange rate of $4.86 US dollars. This level made British exports more expensive on markets across the world and industries tried to cut their costs by lowering worker's wages. It was in this atmosphere of poverty created by these financial adjustments that the grandfather of the third generation Williams cousins, Adrian, Brian and Howard, directors of Cattlegate Farm, left his native Wales and brought his two cows to Kings Cross, London to start a modest milk delivery business.

By 1928 grandfather and grandmother Williams had secured a 300 acre farm in Enfield, just north of the railway line that crosses Crews Hill, where they kept sheep and a small dairy herd. In the mid-1960s the second generation of Williams had taken over the farm and with six working horses had converted the business to arable production. Interestingly one of their first customers was Kenneth Reynolds Wright, father of David Wright of Wright's Mill, Ponders End. The Wrights took grain from the farm for flour production.

Over the years the Williams family have managed to keep afloat by continually changing their business model to compete with evolving consumer habits, they have also needed to protect their business from the extreme pressures of increasing material costs. The Williams family were always on the lookout to improve the profitability of their business and as adjacent land became available, they acquired it and now own some 2000 acres of arable farmland. For a time, land was allotted to the Ford Motor Company for vehicle storage and for 25 years the farm was run as a pick your own and ready-picked soft fruit business until this market finally declined.

Dad and uncle Williams

Cattlegate Farm – Dad (in the foreground) with farm equipment

Cattlegate Farm mint harvesting

Cattlegate Farm biogas plant under construction

Cattlegate Farm tractor fleet

This provoked the enterprising Williams to take on a new business venture and the farm was turned over to herb growing and herb processing. The current main crop is mint and they also bring in horseradish from growers in Norfolk. Like the author, I doubt if many of us, who enjoy a traditional Sunday roast of beef or lamb, would give Cattlegate Farm a second thought as we pile on the horseradish or mint sauce!

In 1988 a long-distance transport haulage and storage firm was established which worked closely with regional and national grain merchants, transporting grains, seeds, animal feeds and fertilisers throughout the United Kingdom and also into Northern Europe. The model for the business is forward looking and designed to be environmentally friendly. When the opportunities arise, small loads from a range of different customers are consolidated by placing them on one large lorry to conserve road miles, which helps to reduce dangerous CO_2 emissions. The firm also ensures that it meets strict health and hygiene regulations for both bulk and curtain-sided vehicles and has introduced a rolling programme of vehicle renewal and upgrading that keeps it in compliance with the latest emission regulations.

In the fast-flowing world of modern-day business it is important that owners invest and innovate to stay alive and ahead of the field. Risk is sometimes an important factor in the staying-alive economy, but as the word suggests, it is clearly an unknown

Cattlegate Farm old milk van

Cattlegate compost made from parks and garden green waste

Cattlegate Farm biogas plant   *Cattlegate Farm, mint processing shed*

factor, and often, if one makes an unconsidered and hasty decision, which turns out to be wrong, the company can end up bankrupt.

By 2008 the three Williams cousins, clearly influenced by their environmentally friendly credentials and with an eye on a sustainable future, began to evaluate the possibility of installing a food waste fed anaerobic digestion facility (anaerobic digestion is an oxygen-free process that can take unwanted food products and turn them into useful biofuels and electricity and can be thought of as a method of carbon capture and CO_2 reduction).

As mentioned above, this new business venture could prove to be an extremely risky move for the Williams if the necessary painstaking research was not fully carried out. However, the cousins diligently set about investigating such important questions as, whether there were sufficient and continuing levels of food waste available within a reasonable mile radius of Cattlegate Farm that would meet their carbon friendly criteria, if so, could the building of an anaerobic digestion plant provide the cousins with a profitable and sustainable business that could be passed onto the next generation? These were important questions and the answers had to be based on the best available knowledge. Therefore, not leaving their own researches to chance, the cousins called in independent consultants to scrutinise their findings and also asked them to provide expert advice. Firms such as Foresight Group LLP, a leading independent infrastructure and private equity investment manager were contacted, along with the respected BDO one of the world's largest accountancy business and advisory companies and also Xergi, a specialist designer and builder of biogas plants who already had some fifty successful installations under its belt.

Harvesting mint at Cattlegate Farm, Enfield

The Williams family, owners of Cattlegate Farm, Enfield

As the feedback from these firms and consultants seemed positive a detailed planning application was made to the relevant authorities for the installation of an anaerobic digestion facility at the farm along with a further application to increase the capacity of the on-site green waste plant from 5,000 tons to 25,000 tons per annum. By the beginning of 2012 planning permission for both facilities had been granted and an independent company, Willen Biogas, was formed to manage and complete the project without interfering with the farm's core herb business. Water runoff from the new facilities is harvested and used for crop irrigation making the farm as self-sufficient as possible.

Now (2018) that the plant is fully up and running, 50,000 tons of local organic material, made up of food and garden waste, is diverted away from landfill sites and used to make electricity for the farm with the surplus being passed to the National Grid. The biogas plant produces 1.5 megawatts of electricity per hour which is enough to power 2,600 homes each year. Leftover waste from the anaerobic digestion process is turned into natural chemical-free fertilisers to be used on the farm and is also sold to other agriculture and horticultural businesses.

Of course, investing in all these new facilities did not come cheap and £7.5 million in financing was obtained from the Green Investment Bank (GIB), a facility set up in November 2012 with £3.8 billion of funding from the UK Government. This is the first bank of its kind in the world which is operated on a "for profit" basis for the express purpose of helping to expedite a faster transition to a greener economy in the UK.

When considering the climate change deniers and also those countries around the world that still rely heavily on fossil fuels for their economic wealth and energy sources, much against the advice of people like Sir David Attenborough, we must think ourselves exceptionally lucky to have the Williams cousins helping to fight global warming right on London's doorstep.

References
Goulding, Tom, *Willen Biogas News* (November 2014)
Interview with Williams cousins and visit to Cattlegate Farm (September 2018)

TWO LUMPS BY THE RIVER THAMES

Not strictly in the Lea Valley but situated within the River Lea's ancient flood-plain is an industry that has stood the test of time. Over the years many people from the London Borough of Newham and beyond have earned their living, and in fact still do today, from two large plants by the River Thames owned by Tate & Lyle, Britain's only cane sugar refiners. However, it is probably fair to conclude that many who live in the area are not fully aware as to why these two factories became established at east and west Silvertown. To learn a little of the history of the company we will need to begin by visiting both Liverpool and Scotland to become acquainted with the backgrounds of the founding fathers, Henry Tate and Abram Lyle.

Henry Tate (who was later knighted, becoming Sir Henry Tate) was born at Chorley, Lancashire in 1819 the son of a Unitarian minister, the Reverend William Tate. Young Henry was apprenticed to his older brother Caleb in the grocery trade, where he appears to have done exceptionally well. At the age of 20 he had set up as a grocer on his own account and by 36 he had established a chain of six shops in the Liverpool area.

It is probable that Tate's later association with sugar derived from his knowledge of the grocery business where his shops would have handled a considerable quantity of the product. In those early days sugar was not the pure white substance that we liberally spoon into our tea and coffee today. Sugar was delivered, after processing, to the retail trade in rather unappetising greyish looking blocks or loaves. The grocer would sell small quantities of these loaves to his customers by chopping off suitably sized chunks. Perhaps Tate thought that he could produce a better-quality product. In any event, in 1859, he went into partnership with John Wright, a sugar refiner of Manesty Lane, Liverpool. Two years after becoming involved with the manufacturing side of the sugar industry, Tate appears to have decided on a new business strategy. In 1861, Tate sold his chain of grocery shops and the following year he opened, on his own account, what has been described as a "small refinery" in Earle

A German Hesser Machine used for packing sugar automatically

Abram Lyle (1820-1891)

Hesser Girl. So called, as in 1920, women were employed to operate the German Hesser sugar packing machines

A Tate & Lyle Thames Lighter passing Tower Bridge

Street, Liverpool. The association with John Wright was dissolved in 1869 and the firm of Henry Tate and Sons was established, when two of his sons, Alfred and Edwin, were taken into partnership. Construction of a new refinery began at Love Lane, Liverpool in 1870 and by 1872 the plant was in production, having an early capacity of 400 tons per week.

Henry Tate, by all accounts, was always on the lookout for new production processes and techniques to make an improved product for the marketplace. He had heard of a method of producing sugar in cube form, patented by Eugen Langen in Germany. In 1875 Tate, in collaboration with David Martineau (a British sugar refiner of Huguenot decent), bought the rights to the process for the British Isles. It is probable that this inspired acquisition of an innovative production process gave Tate the confidence to move to the next stage in his business strategy.

Known as Tate's Army the factory company of Home Guard the Second World War

Lyle's Plaistow refinery c1907. The barrels in the foreground were probably used for storing golden syrup

In about 1875 Henry Tate went to London in search of an opportunity to expand his sugar refining business. He eventually purchased a redundant shipyard on the Thames marshes at Silvertown that had previously been owned by the shipbuilders, Campbell, Johnson & Company. At the time, Tate's purchase was considered to be somewhat foolhardy and amongst some it was thought that the initiative might turn out to be something of a white elephant. This notion may have been influenced by the actions of some Continental beet refiners who had begun exporting sugar to Britain, which could be sold below cost. Their actions were to eventually cause several bankruptcies within the British sugar refining industry. One of the casualties of the Continental dumping was the Silvertown refiner James Duncan of Clyde Wharf, who was forced to close his business in 1886. However, despite the reservations of a few, Tate built his new refinery and production commenced in June 1878. Henry Tate sent his son Edwin and also a Mr J. P. Muir and a Mr J. W. MacDonald to run the Silvertown plant. The latter two men had gained considerable experience of the sugar industry through previously working at refineries in both Liverpool and Scotland.

Sir Henry Tate (1819-1899)

Abram Lyle the third, was born in Scotland in December 1820. His father, also Abram was a cooper and a fishing boat owner. When young Abram was only 12 he went to work for the law firm of James W. Turner. After only two years at the firm Abram decided that the law was not for him and he followed his father into the family business, eventually becoming a cooper and a ship owner.

In 1849 Abram's father died with debts of £7000, leaving the young man to pick up the pieces. Abram got the business back into solvency by first obtaining a loan and then working extremely hard to increase the revenue from cooperage. By the mid-1850s his hard work and dedication had paid off as he had settled his father's debts, paid back the loan and increased his fleet of ships.

The maritime part of the Lyle business had involved the transportation of sugar. It would therefore seem reasonable to assume that the experience that Abram had gained in handling this particular cargo had resulted in his later association and interest in this product. In 1865, along with four partners, Lyle bought the Glebe Sugar Refinery at Greenock. After only seven years Lyle's great friend and principal partner died and he therefore decided to sell his share of the Glebe. He then began to look for other openings in the sugar refining business that offered potential.

Tate & Lyle Thames Refinery today

While it would have probably been less costly for Lyle to have stayed in Scotland and invested once more in the refining industry, he decided that London offered greater commercial opportunities and he would therefore move south to seek his fortune.

In 1881, Lyle purchased two adjacent sites by the Thames amounting to about 11 acres and known as Odam's and Plaistow Wharves. The two sites had been used respectively for the storage of chemical manure and petroleum and would now become the home for Lyle's new London refinery. Lyle's new plant would be built

just over a mile upriver from Tate's refinery at Silvertown. Lyle sent his sons Abram (the fourth) and Charles to oversee the erection and commissioning of the new refinery and a special train was laid-on to take around 400 Greenock men to help with the erection and then the operation of the new facility when it was finally built. The men's families also accompanied them on the train to London.

With a loan of £100,000 from the Bank of Scotland to complete the work, Lyle ensured that his refinery was designed not just to handle the manufacture of sugar but also the production of golden syrup. The plant, technically advanced for its day, came on stream in 1883 and was known as Abram Lyle and Sons. Initially things did not go smoothly for the new facility as the raw sugar market had become decidedly shaky due to Continental manufacturers dumping beet sugar (mentioned earlier). The timing of this had a considerable knock-on effect for Lyle's new business and his first-year losses amounted to £30,000. This loss, along with the loan from the Bank of Scotland, must have put the company under considerable financial pressure. However, no doubt due to a combination of good housekeeping, a loyal workforce and wise management both Abram Lyle and Sons and their competitors, Henry Tate and Sons were able to survive their initial start-up difficulties in, what had become, an unstable market for sugar products.

The Great War (1914-1918) while bringing carnage, misery, mayhem and destruction to Europe had ironically given the sugar refining industry in Britain an unexpected boost. On the Continent much of the agricultural land, which had been used for the cultivation of sugar beet, had been temporarily rendered useless due to the thousands of tons of high explosives that had rained down on it. Therefore, by the end of the conflict, with the European beat sugar producers in severe difficulties, the threat of cheap imports coming to Britain in the immediate future had vanished. Demand on the British sugar industry dramatically increased, which was of considerable benefit to the two Thames refiners, giving them collectively over 50 per cent of the British market. There was also the added benefit that after the war there was a great reluctance, within government circles, to favour the importation of foreign goods to those of indigenous manufacturer and this also helped to place both Tate and Lyle in a commanding position within the industry.

Tate's Thames Refinery c1908

Over the years, while there had been a fair amount of rivalry between the two Thames refineries there does appear to have been, consciously or otherwise, some sort of business understanding that only Tate would manufacture sugar cubes and only Lyle would produce golden syrup. It was probably this unwritten understanding and the commanding position that both companies held in the marketplace that would eventually pave the way to amalgamation. This finally came on 27th February 1921 when the now more familiar name of Tate & Lyle was created. Interestingly the amalgamation apparently did not immediately stop company rivalry as long serving employees were referred to either as "Tate-men" or as "Lyle-men" and the refineries were separately known as "Tateses" and "Lyleses".

The joining of Tate and Lyle, affectionately referred to internally as "the year of the ampersand", brought expansion of both beet and cane sugar refining, modernisation and also the acquisition of a number of small refiners. To cope with the expanding business, and also to revolutionise the way in which sugar was sold, automated packaging machinery was purchased from Hesser of Stuttgart, Germany. The machinery could put sugar into pre-weighed printed cartons for sale by retailers. This was a big advantage over traditional methods of sugar distribution to the shops in sacks, saving the retailer valuable time in weighing and bagging individual amounts for his customers. For the day the Hesser machines were leading edge technology and can probably be compared to today's robots.

In 1936, as the result of a government report, the British Sugar Corporation was formed and the four sugar beet factories that were jointly owned by Tate & Lyle since amalgamation were merged into it. This caused the directors of the company to look towards securing long-term future supplies in case problems arose with the new set-up and, relatively swiftly, cane sugar companies were acquired in Jamaica and Trinidad. By 1939, just prior to the Second World War, the Thames Refinery at Silvertown had become the largest cane sugar refinery in the world and was producing 14,000 tons per week. At the same time the refinery at Liverpool was producing 10,000 tons and Plaistow (Silvertown west) 8,500 tons.

Women posing on the packing line with a box of Tate cube sugar placed in a prominent position

During the war not only did the East End community suffer from nightly bombing raids by the Luftwaffe but also production was affected at the Tate & Lyle refineries when they received several direct hits, as the enemy targeted the London docks. Sugar rationing, suspension of exports and enemy action against merchant shipping caused further reductions in output during this period. However, in keeping with many other manufacturers with a skilled workforce, spare factory capacity was transferred to maintaining the Allied war effort, which resulted in Tate & Lyle producing specialist jigs and fixtures for aircraft like the Lancaster Bomber and Spitfire that became the backbone of the Royal Air Force.

In 1949, three years after the cessation of hostilities, the directors of the company were becoming concerned that the recently elected Labour Government, under Clement Attlee, were preparing to nationalise key industries and this would probably have included sugar. A campaign was quickly mounted to maintain the company's independent status and an artist was commissioned (Bobby St John Cooper) who drew a cartoon character called Mr Cube to promote the anti-nationalisation message. Mr Cube featured on posters, on packaging in newspapers and, in general, anywhere the message could be put across. The campaign, strongly supported by the popularity of Mr Cube, was a success and Tate & Lyle maintained its independent status.

The economic boost that had been given to the British post-war sugar industry by the lifting of rationing restrictions in 1953 had begun to tail off towards the end of the decade. This encouraged the Tate & Lyle directors to look abroad for opportunities of expansion and refiners along with allied industries were acquired around the world. Today, the company, a global leader in carbohydrate processing, has been honed and streamlined around its core business, which has produced an impressive product range.

Tate & Lyle is very much part of the Newham community being one of the largest employers in the area. The company has maintained an impressive historic archive and these facilities are regularly made available to local schools as part of a curriculum development programme. Here children, through site visits and outreach programmes, learn about the many aspects of the sugar refining industry, which has brought prosperity to the region. No doubt the founding fathers, Henry Tate and Abram Lyle, would be justly proud of the way in which their respective Companies have weathered the turbulent economic storms of the past century and a half through a programme of amalgamation, expansion and good management, supported by a loyal workforce. In 2010 Tate & Lyle sold its European Sugars business to American Sugar Refining Incorporated (ASR Group), this included the UK's Tate & Lyle consumer sugar brand and Lyle's Golden Syrup. However, apart from articles about the sale in the business press, it is doubtful if the consumer noticed the transition.

References

Betteridge, Victoria (editor), *Tate & Lyle, 75 Years of Sweet Success*, Tate & Lyle, Bromley, Kent (1996)

Guyver, Eileen (Communications Officer Tate & Lyle Europe), interview (February 2002)

Hugill, Antony, *Sugar and All That, A History of Tate & Lyle*, Gentry Books, London

Lewis, Frank, *Essex and Sugar, Historic and Other Connections*, Phillimore & Co. Ltd, Chichester (1976)

Lyle, Oliver, *The Plaistow Story*, Tate & Lyle Ltd, London (1960)

Powell. W. R. (editor.), *The Victoria History of the County of Essex, Vol. 6*, Institute of Historical Research, University of London (1973)

Sainsbury, Frank, *West Ham 1886-1986*, Council of the London Borough of Newham (1986)

PART THREE

(THE NEW AND THE RELATIVELY NEW KIDS ON THE FOOD AND DRINK BLOCK)

"YES, I COULD DO IT BETTER" – THE STORY OF A LEA VALLEY GROWER

How many of us have heard someone make that claim or, thought that thought about ourselves, but when reality kicks in for one reason or another, we shy away from tackling the task? I call it the "football syndrome". When viewing from the side-lines or from the comfort of an armchair, we criticise a player, manager, or referee for making what we consider to be the wrong decision, as we think we really know better! However, if we were to be put in the position of player, manager or referee we would probably make a complete mess of things. So, you might be surprised to learn that in my researches for this book I did find a man who made the "I could do it better" claim and actually did it much better.

The story begins in Sicily after the Second World War. In 1952 Angelo Russo, the eldest of six children, left his homeland and boarded a train to make a three-day journey across Europe to England. At the time in Sicily food was in short supply with many people starving and employment opportunities extremely rare. With little chance of things improving in the foreseeable future Angelo made the decision to leave his family and his country behind to seek a better life. He had been sponsored by a British manufacturer of concrete lampposts to come to England on a four-year work permit. This was under a government initiative that was intended to help rebuild the country and get Britain back onto its feet after the devastation of towns, cities and the transport infrastructure that had occurred during the Second World War. The conditions of the four-year permits were particularly strict and immigrants on arrival had to register with the police, provide proof of financial support, have the backing of a UK resident and remain with the same employer for the four-year period. Failing to comply meant that the permit would be revoked and immigrants would be required to return to their home country. Despite the harshness of the 1919 Aliens Act and also the 1920 Aliens Order, in the early post-war period, many people from overseas, who had been encouraged to take up Britain's offer of work, remained and helped rebuild the country.

After two years Angelo had saved enough money to bring his wife to England and by the late 1950s two children were born, Jimmy and Vince. Angelo had long held the

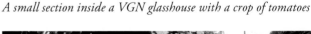

Cucumbers being prepared at VGS pack house   *A small section inside a VGN glasshouse with a crop of tomatoes*

Aerial view of Nazeing VGS site

vision of working for himself and, no doubt, prompted by the birth of his children, the dream now took on extra urgency. Amazingly, by 1963, he had scraped together enough money to put a down-payment on a small and failing, coal-fired nursery, situated on three-quarters of an acre of land at Wormley in Hertfordshire. This is thought to be the first purchase of a nursery by a Sicilian or an Italian immigrant. Here Angelo and his wife Angela worked singlehandedly growing cucumbers that were sold to the London markets of Covent Garden and Spitalfields. As Jimmy and Vince grew up the boys helped out in the nursery during school holidays and also at weekends but, like most young people, they never really became interested in working for their parents.

By the 1980s Jimmy and Vince were working for a salad and vegetable wholesaler, S.V. Salads. Jimmy as a sales representative and Vince as a driver. Here the brothers worked for around three years and it was at this company that Jimmy got his "I can do it better" moment. In 1982 the brothers acquired a small building at Roydon, Essex and began selling locally sourced horticultural produce to general retail outlets at competitive prices. Soon, Jimmy realised that the business could not survive if it continued at its current rate of expansion and in his words, "I needed to take life to another level". By 1985 he had raised the necessary finance to acquire what is now Valley Grown Salads (VGS) and expand the site into a first class produce arrivals, incoming produce inspection, produce packing and labelling, produce distribution and administration facility. Considerable investment was also made into creating a purpose-built transport fleet to serve VGS's growing customer base.

Early image of VGS fork-lift driver loading

Jimmy Russo left and Vince Russo right, joint owners of VGS and VGN

Jimmy and Vince Russo's father

Jimmy and Vince Russo's mother

The initiative was an instant success and in 1986 VGS began supplying cucumbers to Presto supermarkets. Two years later VGS began serving Waitrose, part of the John Lewis Partnership, with cucumbers and in 1991 this was followed with peppers and the following year aubergines were being shipped. However, although the business was now turning over nicely, Jimmy and his brother soon realised that to survive in a highly competitive market one must constantly be on the lookout for new opportunities and sometimes be prepared to take risks. In 1999 Langridge Nursery in Paynes Lane, Nazeing was acquired. Now the Russo brothers had done something which they had vowed never to do; they had become growers!

Clearly, they must have known what they wanted and were planning for the long-term future of their overall business before they took on this new project as it was obvious before the start that further investment would be required. This was to see the building of the latest aluminium-framed glasshouses, construction of new canteen and toilet facilities for staff.

As the science of heating modern glasshouses economically was changing the brothers took the sensible decision to wait and review the technology so as not to miss the best options that were appearing on the horizon. If they had chosen to immediately install the currently available state-of-the-art combined heat and power system (CHP) this could have proved to be an expensive mistake. A modern gas-fired heating system was installed to tide them over, replacing the existing oil-fired system. Apart from improving the nursery's overall growing efficiency the investment brought about an immediate lowering of the site's carbon dioxide (CO_2) footprint by removing an expensive fossil fuel source.

The new acquisition now became Valley Grown Nurseries (VGN) which operates a strict system of quality control. No produce grown at the nursery can be shipped directly to the customer. It must first be sent to VGS at Roydon where all the quality checks are carried out before packaging, labelling and shipment to the customer. In

2004, for monitoring and maintaining these high quality and growing standards, VGN received the coveted award "UK Salad Grower of the Year".

Trying to follow the progress of the Russo brothers, now that they have become growers, is like trying to keep up with Usain Bolt in the 200 metres Olympic final! In 2000, to maintain year-round supplies of produce for their customers, outside of the UK's growing season, VGS invested in their supply bases in Israel and Spain. Four years later in 2004 a new pack house was built at Roydon to handle tomatoes. 2005 saw more investment at VGN, Nazeing with the installation of the hanging gutter system. This is effectively many lines of extremely long shelves suspended above the ground on wire braces connected to the glasshouse frame. On these shelves rest rows and rows of individual plant containers, rather like growbags, filled with a rock-wool fibre mixture rather than earth; each plant being automatically fed with the correct amount of nutrients and water by a computer-controlled system. The growing of plants using mineral nutrients in water without soil is known as hydroponics and has a number of economic advantages. One of these is better control of pests and diseases which can lay dormant in soil and cause havoc for the grower.

Following the Russo brothers' progress, now that they had become growers, has highlighted the new skills they have learned and taken on. To ensure that they keep their existing customers happy and also with a view to attract prospective new clients they began introducing trials of produce so that the consumer could experience a wide choice of salads with subtle and improved flavours. In 2006 commercial trials of Sicilian cucumbers began, followed, in 2007, by the introduction of Padron peppers and in 2008 Sicilian peppers were trialled. Following extensive trials in 2010 new tomato varieties were launched for that year's winter season. 2011 saw red Lamuya peppers launched and in the following year sweet baby red peppers were introduced followed, in 2014, with sweet Cherie tomatoes.

These rapid introductions of new produce reminded the author of a mantra, already mentioned in the chapter about H. Forman and Sons, which he preaches to new business studies students; *"just when you believe that your business is most successful, that is when the business is most vulnerable"*. In other words, never ever take your eyes off the ball! Business students wishing to find a case study of how to run a successful business in a highly competitive market segment would do well to choose a company like VGS.

The popularity of these new products had increased consumer demand which in turn had put pressure on VGN, the growing arm of VGS, and in 2015 work

New VGN glasshouse under construction

commenced on phase one of a £10 million project. This was to add 12 acres of glasshouse buildings, followed by phase two adding a further ten acres of glass to the existing glasshouses giving the VGN Nazeing site an overall glass footprint of 30 acres. The building programme also accommodated warehousing, an environmentally friendly system of water harvesting and modern staff facilities.

However, prior to the above construction taking place, there had been two unsuccessful planning submissions, but Jimmy and Vince's persistence paid off and permission was finally approved for the build. Unfortunately,

New VGN glasshouses completed

the Lee Valley Regional Park Authority (LVRPA) decided to fight the plans in the Court of Appeal on the grounds that the development would have a negative impact on wildlife and be detrimental to a green belt area. Eventually the LVRPA conceded that the National Planning Policy Framework did after all allow for sustainable agricultural development within the park.

The eventual result seemed like a victory for common sense, particularly when every day we are encouraged by the authorities to eat more fresh food and maintain a healthy lifestyle to help fight obesity and associated diseases. It is thought that the benefits resulting from this healthier lifestyle regime will be a win-win situation by releasing pressures on our overworked NHS. Also, scientists are currently reporting growing concerns about the rapid increase in global warming as daily we witness the tragic effects of this through footage on our television screens. Here we see communities being devastated by drought, forest fires, landslides, polar ice sheets melting, rising sea levels, coastal erosion, flooding, tsunamis and hurricanes. All this makes the need for more fresh home-grown produce even greater to lessen the number of miles our food has to travel (food miles) and help reduce the effects of our Earth's carbon footprint (the emission of CO_2 and other noxious gasses).

The new VGN glasshouses were constructed in partnership with the Bom Group, a major Netherlands based designer, developer and constructor of state-of-the-art award-winning glasshouses. This particular set of glasshouses are the first of their kind in the UK. Ambient light transmission to the plants is paramount within the design. This has been achieved by making the supporting structure as narrow as possible to give maximum illumination of some 91 per cent. The glasshouse is designed to withstand the vagaries of the British weather with tempered glass panes in the roof while special patented wind-bracing connections hold the whole structure together. The latest design of low-NOx temperature-controlled boiler, connected to a four million litre heat storage tank, provides the necessary heat for the glasshouses at times when the sun is not shining.

Rainwater is collected from the glasshouse roofs and gutters and stored in a large outside lake which is now attracting birds and wildlife to the site. This stored water is treated and fed back through an irrigation system to feed the plants. In times of drought the nursery can rely on abstracted ground-water from its own private bore-hole, making the site self-sufficient.

2016 saw the first year of growing in the 12 acre phase one VGN glasshouse followed, in 2017, by the ten acre phase two glasshouse with a speciality crop of Axiany, a variety of tomato renowned for its excellent flavour.

I think the reader will agree that the 32 year journey (1986-2018) from salad distributor to salad grower, is a truly remarkable achievement for Jimmy and Vince Russo and they clearly haven't finished yet. They are both aware of the constant need to improve growing efficiency and also to develop new salad varieties for the ever-changing tastes of the consumer. All this has to be done in an atmosphere of a highly competitive marketplace that makes high demands of the growers, squeezing tighter and tighter their slender profit margins.

Discussing the above with Jimmy he makes the point that "food is generally too cheap". To back up his argument he gives the following example. "Consider the journey of a yellow Brazilian melon that retails in Tesco for £1-49. It's grown by a farmer thousands of miles away, picked by the farmer, put in a box then transported to the docks then transferred to a shipping container. The container is shipped to the UK where it gets unloaded and then the melon is re-packaged and labelled then sent to the supermarket where it gets put on a shelf. How much does it cost to post a letter to Brazil"? Jimmy leans back in his seat after a point well made.

The author asked Jimmy what measures he would like to see the government taking that would help the UK growing industry become more profitable. I also asked how the next generation of growers could be encouraged to create a sustainable and self-sufficient agricultural and horticultural industry that does not rely on imports. His wish list is as follows:

- Tax breaks and grants that would help growers invest in long-term modernisation and expansion projects

- Campaigns to encourage healthy eating

- An increase to the minimum wage to a living wage level

- A long-term programme for environmental improvement linked to a joined-up low carbon energy policy

Part of the modern VGS transport fleet

Pepper sorting and packing at a VGN pack house

The author would agree that Jimmy's requests should be considered seriously at government level if we really wish to have a thriving, self-sustaining horticultural and agricultural industry in the UK. Unfortunately, governments only appear to operate on a five-year window and long-term sustainable strategies are ignored. Perhaps it is time for politicians to settle their differences so that long-term policies could be mutually agreed that would last beyond the five-year election term!

The challenge has been laid down; which political party will be brave enough to pick up the gauntlet?

References

Correspondence and telephone conversation with Francesca Russo, Accounts Assistant, VGS (September 2018)

Interview and correspondence with Jimmy Russo (joint owner VGS and VGN) (September 2018)

Interview and correspondence with Vince Russo (joint owner VGS and VGN) (September 2018)

Lewis, Jim, *A Century of Growing the History of the Lea Valley Growers' Association from 1911 to 2011*, Libri Publishing Ltd, London (2011)

Note

Since the Russo brother's parents first took over a failing British small nursery in the 1960s, the current (2019) Lea Valley glasshouse industry has changed out of all recognition. Italian and Sicilian families were invited to come to the UK to help revive a struggling horticultural industry that was haemorrhaging local labour in the post-war period. The second generation of these families now own and manage around 80-90 per cent of the Lea Valley glasshouse industry.

HOW WOULD WE SURVIVE WITHOUT IMMIGRANTS AND THEIR DESCENDANTS?

When taking a lunch break, sitting down to our evening meal, phoning for a take-away or going to a restaurant how often do we consider who has grown, processed, cooked and prepared the food we eat? The answer is, probably not very often.

In my research for this book it has become patently clear, even within the relatively small geographic region of the Lea Valley, that, without the help of today's immigrants who work in our food and hospitality industries, we would find it extremely difficult to feed ourselves. The story that is about to unfold is about a young boy who came to this country with his parents in the 1960s. What he eventually made of himself is almost unbelievable.

Mustafa Kiamil, a Turkish Cypriot, came to the UK as a 13-year-old with his parents in 1963 to escape the serious military tensions in his homeland between Turk and Greek. The family settled in Palmers Green, Enfield where Mustafa, like many local boys of his age, took to riding his bicycle on journeys of discovery throughout the Lea Valley region. During one of these adventures he came upon Rammey Marsh, Enfield, part of which was an old dumping ground where people used to illegally fly-tip their rubbish. Amongst the rubbish he found discarded cycles, cycle frames, wheels, handlebars and chains and he would strap what pieces he could carry to his back and return home with them. After several return journeys he had enough parts to assemble a few bicycles, and then with a can of spray paint his handiwork got brightened up into something presentable. These creations where then sold to eager buyers looking for a bargain and behold, a young entrepreneur was born.

After leaving school at 16 Mustafa spent the next five years studying Radio & Televising Engineering at Southgate Technical College receiving his City & Guilds certificates. At college he was inspired by his tutor to become a better engineer and Mustafa took a job as a service engineer with Granada Television Rentals, repairing anything from transistor radios to colour television receivers. When Granada decided to scrap their ageing Grundig televisions and replace them with the latest Fergusons, Mustafa saw a golden opportunity. He quickly bought ten faulty Grundig models for a song and made six working televisions out of them, selling them on for a handsome profit. It was now becoming clear that the bicycle selling period was not a boyish fluke and the maturing Mustafa was really turning into a hard-nosed and seasoned business entrepreneur.

After marriage to Fatima whose family had connections in the restaurant business, Mustafa, always the budding entrepreneur, got the idea of opening his own burger bar which he did in 1982, naming it Jenny's, after his wife's anglicised name. Over the next six years Mustafa grew the business into a popular London restaurant chain.

While running his burger bars Mustafa had encountered difficulties sourcing good quality food products from reliable suppliers and, once again, this set him thinking. His logic told him that if he had faced problems obtaining supplies of the right quality and price, delivered on time, then other restaurant outlets would have had similar disappointing experiences. In 1988, not averse to taking risks, Mustafa's next

From fish and chips to toilet rolls, you name it JJ Foods has it

Chiller cabinets containing JJ Foods products

Goods waiting in JJ Foods loading bay awaiting collection

venture was to set up his own food distribution centre in a modest 3,000 square feet building in Hornsey, North London. The business being named JJ Food Services.

It would seem that Mustafa's sensitive nose for business opportunities had sniffed out a gap in the market and by applying a formula, dreamed up out of his earlier poor experiences, he was soon supplying a range of cafes, takeaways, coffee shops and quick service restaurants across North London. The Hornsey business became an instant success and over the next few years seven new food and drink distribution centres were opened in strategic locations: Basingstoke, Bristol, Birmingham, Doncaster, Leeds, Manchester and Sidcup.

Over the years Mustafa's thoughts often turned to pleasant boyhood memories of his early days in England, when he would ride his bicycle to Rammey Marsh to collect those discarded old bike parts and he was suddenly taken by a strong urge. Against colleague advice, he secured a parcel of land on Innova Business Park, Enfield, the former dumping ground of the bicycle parts, and here Mustafa built his head office and food and drink distribution centre. Technology plays a vital part of JJ Food's business with online ordering proving very popular with customers. At the time of writing online orders account for 63 per cent of the business. Other modern buying

Mustafa Kiamil, CEO and founder of JJ Foods with Grocer Gold Award, one of many received

JJ Foods company owned transport fleet, Enfield

JJ Foods security gate, Enfield

habits are catered for via a JJ Food's App which allows customers to shop anytime, anywhere and on the go. No doubt Mustafa's early electronic engineering training at Southgate Technical College has played a crucial part in the way the business has embraced technology to support turnover.

A recent sourcing and supply chain agreement with Unique Seafood, a respected industry company, has enabled JJ Food's to offer a consistent range of high quality and competitively priced fish and seafood products to its customers. By the time this book is published I would have expected JJ Food's to have substantially increased its outlets across the UK and also its range of customer offers.

The thoughtful progress of JJ Food's service to its customers and the investment in technology had not gone unnoticed by leading industry sources as the company won an array of prestigious awards. In 2015 JJ Food's scooped the Microsoft Big Data & Insights Award and was listed in the Sunday Times Top Track 250 as one of the UKs fastest growing small and medium sized enterprises (SMEs). In 2016 the business won the Grocer's Technology Supplier of the Year Award.

In July 2018 the author had the privilege of being shown over JJ Food's Enfield facilities by their Group General Manager, Terry Larkin, and was extremely impressed by what he saw. A constant fleet of JJ Food's customer's vans and cars turned up at the multiple-door bays to collect their orders which were dealt with efficiently by operatives using hand-held computers. These operatives dispatched the pre-picked orders to vehicles as they arrived at the various goods bays and then issued the correct paperwork to the departing customers. This was a well-oiled and slick operation that went like clockwork.

Mustafa must have clearly understood that any business can only perform well if the staff enjoy good working conditions. On the author's travels around the distribution

Typical JJ Foods product catalogue

Loading vehicles at JJ Foods Enfield warehouse

Terry Larkin in high-vis jacket,
Group General Manager JJ Foods

centre he saw modern staff canteen facilities and rest areas and also witnessed a young child who was being kept amused during the school holidays while his mother was working. Outside in the yard were some of JJ Food's transport fleet which are totally owned and maintained by the company.

In the author's experience of working in industry around the world I have never experienced a business which has developed so rapidly and efficiently as JJ Food Service, while at the same time making an enormous effort to research and understand its customer needs in detail and implemented the necessary systems to give them the services they wanted. It is particularly refreshing when one remembers that this formula for success has come from the brain of a 13-year old immigrant boy who clearly had a vision and a nose for business!

References
Interview and correspondence with Mustafa Kiamil (CEO, JJ Food Service) (September 2018)

Site visit and interview with Terry Larkin (Group General Manager, JJ Food Service)

WARBURTONS – ENFIELD'S LARGEST BAKER, MAKER OF THE UK'S MOST POPULAR BREAD

The wholly owned family firm of Warburtons was founded in 1876 when Ellen and Thomas Warburton bought a small grocery shop in the Lancashire town of Bolton in 1876. When they began their enterprise, they could never have imagined, not even in their wildest dreams, how their business would grow in size to produce revenues of over £574 million by the year 2018.

In around 1996 the firm decided on a southern expansion programme which resulted in Warburtons gaining a 24 per cent share of the UK bread market in comparison with two per cent when the business was located solely in Bolton.

During the planning of the expansion programme it was reasoned that if bread products were to reach their customers in other areas of the UK outside of Lancashire, they would have to arrive fresh otherwise market share would be compromised. Part of the expansion programme rationale was to acquire large bakeries in strategic parts of the UK as they went into administration. This gave Warburtons a ready-made bakery that could be updated complete with an experienced workforce. The other part of the plan was to build large regional bakeries that could quickly serve a range of specific satellite towns and areas. In the case of Warburtons Enfield bakery, these were Paddock Wood, Basingstoke, Worthing and the Isle of Wight. In fact, the bakery can proudly boast, that bread baked today can be on their customers' shelves by eight o'clock the following morning.

Visiting the Enfield bakery at Delta Park was a real eye-opener as the scale and cleanliness of bread and associated product production was overwhelming. Entering the cavernous building is like being inside a set of a James Bond movie where futuristic and technologically advanced machines are preparing to conquer the world. Here, at Warburtons, several computer-controlled flow lines snake their way around the building taking the product from the flour-mixing and dough-making stages through the gigantic ovens and onto the quality testing, cooling and cutting areas before being automatically packed and made ready for delivery.

Jonathan Warburton, Chairman (courtesy Warburtons)

Plaque to commemorate the opening of Warburtons Enfield Bakery, unveiled by HRH the Duke of Edinburgh, 2003

Image of bread production at a Warburton bakery (courtesy Warburton)

Warburtons production machinery similar to that installed at the Enfield bakery (courtesy Warburtons)

Warburtons transport at the Enfield bakery

No small detail of bread and product quality is left to chance. Within every flow-line electronic sensors are arranged to pick up the smallest of foreign bodies or other irregularities that might have somehow contaminated the product and if, on a rare occasion, detection occurs, the offending item is immediately rejected. When passing the end of the crumpet ovens the author was allowed to personally test a hot freshly baked crumpet, without the butter of course, and the results were pretty satisfying! Unfortunately, photography or mobile phones were not allowed within the production areas for food safety and security reasons so readers will have to rely on the author's description of the plant when sampling a Warburtons product.

It was interesting to learn that the breadmaking process at the Enfield bakery consumes an incredible four ton of flour per hour, a considerable amount of which is delivered from the nearby Wright's Mill at Ponders End, in keeping with the Warburton policy of reducing road miles. Unlike many other large bakers, Warburtons do not make "own brand" products for the supermarkets, the only exceptions being Weight Watchers bread and an artisan bread for Waitrose. In keeping with modern dietary needs the company also produces a range of gluten-free products.

The Enfield bakery, which was opened by HRH the Duke of Edinburgh in October 2003 employs some 450 people and a second depot in the borough employs a further 200 making Warburtons one of the largest local employers.

Today, many large company transport fleets are contracted out to various logistic groups, but in the case of Warburtons the transport fleet is solely owned by the company, giving them complete control of product movement.

At a time when large companies are often part of an even larger impersonal company grouping, it is refreshing to learn that Warburtons is a wholly-owned fifth-generation family business. It is also reassuring that, in these troubled times when many well-loved companies and brand names are disappearing, the Warburtons dynasty has the sixth generation waiting in the wings to continue the family legacy of a respected familiar brand name.

Note

In recent years Warburtons have spent considerable sums of money on advertising and marketing campaigns that inject light-hearted humour into product publicity. In 2015 they announced that Sylvester Stallone would be re-enacting some of the major parts that he had formerly played. Another campaign involved the Muppets singing the praises of a new giant crumpet. The latest (2018) is a highly amusing piece with northern comedian Peter Kay acting out his Bolton connections in front of Warburtons' chairman, Jonathan Warburton.

References

BBC News, 'Bakery toasts expansion plan' (27th October 2003)

Enfield bakery visit by the author (September 2018)

Teather, Daniel, 'Family Values Hold Key to the Rise and Rise of Warburtons', *The Guardian* (April 2010)

GREGGS – A BAKERY WITH A DIFFERENCE

Greggs, now a familiar name on many of our high streets serving tasty savoury ready to go snacks, cakes and drinks, was established in the north-east of England in 1939 by John Gregg. John set up a door-to-door push-bike bakery round, delivering eggs, bread and associated products to the mining areas around Newcastle upon Tyne. Over the years throughout the company's progression these strong community links, that reach back to the business's working-class origins, have always been maintained.

The Second World War interrupted company growth and it wasn't until 1951 that the first Greggs shop opened on Gosforth High Street, Newcastle purchased for £7,750, a snip at today's prices but reasonably expensive at the time. After John Gregg died in 1964, his eldest son Ian took over the running of the business. Just prior to his father's death, Ian, after graduating from university, and in keeping with his family's wishes, had already begun a professional career working for a firm of Newcastle solicitors. Taking over the family business, which then had 15 staff and a turnover of £70,000, was a leap in the dark for Ian, as he openly admitted that, "I didn't know anything about business or baking, I came with a completely fresh mind and listened carefully to what other people said". This Ian took as a "big benefit" to the business path that he was about to tread.

Once Ian had acquired sufficient business skills, through effectively learning on the job, he began a programme of expansion by first buying bakeries across the north of England, many of which were struggling financially. In 1972 Scotland became the next target when an existing bakery chain was re-branded as Greggs of Rutherglen. The Leeds-based Thurston's came next in 1974 when Greggs took over the established baking chain and re-branded it as Greggs of Yorkshire. This was followed by Broomfield's in London, Bowkett's in Kent and Took's in East Anglia.

Greggs Enfield Bakery

Greggs sandwiches a popular snack on our High Streets (courtesy Greggs)

Greggs early transport fleet (courtesy Greggs)

*Greggs first shop, Gosforth, Newcastle upon Tyne 1951
(courtesy Greggs)*

By 1976 Ian seems to have been a little over-enthusiastic with his recent purchases, as he has readily admitted, "we overstretched ourselves". This was when Greggs bought 100 shops from the failing Manchester-based Price's bakery. For the next eighteen months or so, Greggs had to slow down their rapid pace of expansion until they were able to turn their new acquisitions around. This was done by modernising the shops and successfully introducing a new range of products and services to their Mancunian customers.

In 1983 Ian stepped down from his role as Managing Director after taking the family bakery chain from one single shop to 300 outlets in just 19 years. The company reins were then handed over to Michael Darrington (who was knighted in 2004). Before joining Greggs, Darrington had trained as a chartered accountant and then spent 17 years in various roles with United Biscuits. After attending Harvard Business School, he became part of United's general management team.

Darrington's business style was more cautious than his predecessor, taking the business forward slowly and promoting the value-for-money aspects of their products to their customers. A year after joining Greggs Darrington took the business public, which at the time was valued at £14 million.

In 1994 Greggs seized the opportunity of making a major acquisition when they acquired the chain of Bakers Oven shops from Allied Bakeries, but decided not to change the familiar high street name. However, in 1999, Greggs rebranded the one hundred shops of the earlier acquired Braggs, naming them Greggs of the Midlands.

In the summer of 2008, after 25 years of service, Sir Michael Darrington retired. He had taken the company from 300 to over 1,400 shops and since flotation the share price had climbed to an astonishing 6,000 per cent of the original figure. In 1987, during his stewardship, the charity, the Greggs Trust was established, later becoming the Greggs Foundation, with the aim of putting something back into local communities. The charity has, and continues to raise, millions of pounds for local good causes, including the BBC Children in Need Appeal, and also runs over 400 breakfast clubs, ensuring that thousands of children in under-privileged areas begin the day with a healthy meal.

Greggs sausage rolls, one of their most popular products.
Now a vegan version is available (courtesy Greggs)

Greggs second Enfield facility

Because of Sir Michael's considerable experience, he was encouraged to remain on the Greggs board as a non-executive director. In his retirement Sir Michael took the opportunity to launch a campaign which he labelled "pro-business and anti-greed". An article in *The Guardian* really showed Sir Michael's long-held beliefs, when he explained that he wished to "scotch the myth that attacks on executive rewards are attacks on business". Here he let rip with forthright views, saying, "It is a smoke-screen and a lot of bollocks – it is the greed of people [at the top] that is anti-business." Sir Michael is now seen as one the UK's first senior executives to be highly critical of his peers by attacking boardroom pay in corporate Britain. Sir Michael's views are reflected in the management philosophy of Ian Gregg when he explained that, "There are too many fat cats out there creaming off company profits but that has never been the case at Greggs. We've always looked after our staff first, then our customers, then our shareholders but in a lot of places that's flipped the other way around."

Greggs next Chief Executive, Ken McMeikan, joined the company in June 2008, after a 14 spell with Tesco, running the supermarket's Japanese business before he joined Sainsbury's in 2005. From the choice of someone with the background and experience of Ken McMeikan it was clear that Greggs wanted to take the company forward to a higher level and the new CEO had been particularly chosen to bring in fresh thinking.

One of the first changes that was made to the marketing strategy under his leadership was to take advantage of the company's national advertising programme and, in December 2008, the 165 Bakers Oven shops that had been purchased earlier in 1994 were rebranded as Greggs. This was done to promote Greggs as a national brand and also to increase the level of high street customer familiarity. In 2009, McMeikan, in taking the company forward, announced an ambitious programme to open 500 new shops across the UK, to introduce the selling of frozen sausage rolls, to open outlets in motorway service stations and to launch new up-market cafes.

In 2012 Greggs became the leaders in a campaign against George Osborne's, the then Chancellor of the Exchequer's, proposal to continue and also to allegedly simplify the taxing on certain types of takeaway food. In 1984 Nigel Lawson had introduced a 20 per cent value added tax (VAT) on hot takeaway fast food, while food intended to be cooked and eaten at home was to be kept zero VAT rated. The problem, which particularly concerned Greggs and other bakeries, was that many of their products like sausage rolls, pies and pasties, which are left to cool to around room temperature after preparation, rather being kept hot or reheated, had fallen foul of the Chancellor's legislation.

To outsiders observing the debate in parliament about adding a 20 per cent tax on pasties, and their like, became laughable. During a debate of the Treasury Select Committee the Chancellor was ridiculed for not remembering when he last bought a pasty from Greggs. One Select Committee member, the MP John Mann, highlighted the stupidity of the tax by explaining that a lukewarm pasty would be taxable in cold weather, but not in hot weather, because of different ambient temperatures. This debate of hot pasties being taxed and cold pasties being exempt appeared to many that parliamentarians were suffering from heatstroke! The Chancellor responded by insisting that the "tax made sense, but said the Government would not check the temperature of every pasty sold". No doubt many people slept peacefully in their beds after that night after the Chancellor's statement!

Readers may recall the media frenzy with television news items and newspaper headlines about the "pasty tax" and "Pasty Gate". The whole occasion reminiscent of an episode from *Yes Minister*! After considerable negative publicity and also pressure from MP's, the media, the baking industry and certain retail food outlets, Mr Osbourne did a very swift U-turn.

At the time of writing (2019) Greggs policy of concentrating on the "food on the go" market has made them one of the UK's most profitable and customer-centric high street fast-food retailers. Clearly the company has taken on board the current healthy living ethic by claiming that "… we still pay attention to important things. Like serving food that's free from the nasty stuff [we] don't use artificial colours, flavourings, added trans fats or MSG." In January this year, after considerable product research and recipe testing, Greggs launched a Quorn-filled vegan

Roger Whiteside, CEO Greggs
(courtesy Greggs)

alternative to their popular meat-filled traditional sausage roll in 950 of their 1,950 shops. According to a *Guardian* article Greggs current CEO, Roger Whiteside, is quoted as saying, "Its literally flying off the shelves" then added, "it's the fastest selling new line in the six-years I have been with the company."

Recently Greggs spent £8 million updating their Enfield plant with a state-of-the-art bakery that now employs 240 people and has the capability of producing 18,000 sausage rolls per hour. Currently the plant produces around 1.25 million sausage rolls per week which are supplied daily from depots in Leeds, Birmingham, Treforest and Enfield.

The Enfield distribution centre, which employs around 200 people, currently delivers product to approximately 450 shops in the south-east of England that are located in major towns and in areas around Cambridge, Milton Keynes, Reading, Bournemouth, Folkestone, Margate, Southend, Clacton and Lowestoft.

Normally we hear stories of how it is businesses in the affluent south of England that prosper and then tend to influence those in the north. Therefore, it is refreshing to learn about a genuine northern business that has bucked this market trend!

References

Author unknown, 'The inside story of the rise of Greggs to the top', *The Journal* (25th June 2013)

Bowers, Simon, 'Ex-Greggs chief attacks executive pay', *The Guardian* (22nd February 2012)

Correspondence and phone calls with Havas PR, Manchester, Greggs Account Director

Monaghan, Angela, 'Greggs struggles to keep up with demand for vegan sausage rolls', *The Guardian* (January 2019)

Note

The figures quoted for the Enfield bakeries sausage roll production does not include the new vegan version. At the time of writing the vegan figures are confidential.

SNOWBIRD FOODS – A PRODUCER ON THE SITE OF THE FORMER PONDERS END SHELL WORKS

In researching the Lea Valley's diverse and expanding food production industry the author has been genuinely surprised by the extraordinary things that he has discovered about how some of our everyday food products finally arrive on our plates and these discoveries will probably be a surprise to the reader too. Some of these facts came to light when interviewing Philip Paul, the joint Managing Director of Snowbird Foods, at his Ponders End office in February 2019, and will be revealed in the story that follows.

The company was established on its present site in 1999 and interestingly the plot of land that the factory now occupies was once the home of the Ponders End Shell Works that supplied munitions to the Allied Forces at the time of the Great War (1914-1918). Originally the factory was owned by a food manufacturer in Hackney, East London, Plum Tree Farms, who produced raw sausage and burgers. When the company took over the Ponders End site in 1999, it became a fully cooked sausage and burger manufacturer. Over the following years the business changed hands several times becoming part of the Dutch food group Vion. When Vion decided to withdraw from the UK, the business was acquired by the Karro Foods Group, one of the UK's largest pork producers and processors. As Karro's business was dedicated to raw pork production it was not an easy fit with Snowbird Foods, its new acquisition.

Albert McGovern, the other joint Managing Director of Snowbird Foods with Philip Paul, is responsible for all things financial. In 2013 he was able to put his financial expertise to the test when he negotiated a hard-won management buyout with Karro Foods that crucially allowed the new management team to retain the Snowbird company name. He was also responsible for arranging the necessary finances with the banks on the basis that the directors would also have to contribute some of their own money towards the settlement. Also, part of the tough negotiations saw Snowbird having to put up the plant's modern food production machinery as collateral so that the deal could finally be sealed with Karro.

Industry Awards Highly Commended 2019

Locally sourced outside bred pork for Snowbird sausages

Sausages in the manufacturing process prior to cooking

Snowbird 'bangers' galore!

Snowbird Foods Ponders End, built on the site of the old World War 1 Shell Works. No wonder their 'bangers' are so popular!

Snowbird Foods' joint MDs, Albert McGovern and Philip Paul

Snowbird production operative keeping a hungry machine topped up

When discussing the acquisition with Philip Paul, he explained that while the buyout was a massive decision for the management team, "it's not one that took much thinking about." Over the past few years, Philip and his colleagues, while working for the former owners, had developed and considerably expanded the product range and the staff had felt proud of what they had achieved, which in a way had created a collective feeling of ownership. Furthermore, Philip explained that if Snowbird Foods had not been acquired by the management buyout, the Ponders End plant would have closed and jobs would have inevitability been lost.

Six years on from the buyout, Snowbird are producing around 120 tons of food products a week, while two-thirds of the output are frozen and fully cooked sausages, the following third is made up of various varieties of meatball and a range of other popular foodstuffs that are shipped to ready meals manufacturers, ending up as sandwich fillers and in the familiar branded packs of frozen and microwave meals. Apart from the products reaching the UK's leading supermarket shelves, a great deal of the cooked and frozen foodstuffs are also delivered to hotels, ferry companies and restaurants.

Snowbird Foods have built up an outstanding reputation with UK ready meal manufacturers for producing exceptionally high quality food products. They have achieved this by sourcing meat only from reputable British suppliers with traceable product credentials and they also endeavour to source products as locally as possible to help the environment by minimising food miles. The closest supplier is Wright's

Snowbird meatballs and spaghetti

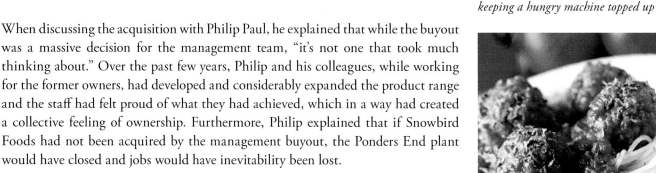

Snowbird sausages, prepared, made and cooked at Ponders End in their thousands

Snowbird Foods logo

Mill at Ponders End, which supply flour, and is almost on their doorstep. Philip Paul admitted that, "their flour is slightly more expensive than other millers, but I have not been able to source a better-quality product".

Each batch of product produced by Snowbird Foods is quarantined by the company before it can be released to the customer. Random samples from the batch are sent to an independent test laboratory for scientific analysis and also to show that the product complies with the list of ingredients and other information on the packaging label. The product is also tested for any unwanted contaminants that could have entered the batch at the production site or may have come in to the site with a shipment from a supplier. Once the laboratory is satisfied with the batch it issues a Certificate of Analysis (COA) that allows Snowbird Foods to release the product to its ready meal customers. Maintaining these strict standards of food safety and high quality has allowed Snowbird Foods to amass, in recent years, no less than 16 industry quality and innovation awards.

When discussing the outlook for the company with Philip Paul the author learned there was considerable enthusiasm for expansion of the plant with the possibility of future business acquisitions. However, Philip did express a note of caution over the current (February 2019) on-going and unresolved negotiations between the UK Government and Brussels that had already cost his company a considerable sum of money. Philip explained that because of the uncertainty about what might happen over the issue of a customs border between the UK and the European Union, he had already, as a precaution, hired an off-site temperature-controlled warehouse to store 600 tons of onions that he had bought, in advance, from Poland. This was to ensure that he could keep his business running in the event of the government's negotiations failing. The onions, that were a crucial component of many of Philip's recipes along with a range of spices, were the only ingredients that he imported from abroad. Without this six-month stock of onions, he could not have guaranteed that his ready meal customers would be able to supply the UK's restaurants, supermarkets, hotels and crucially the NHS. Imagine the chaos that such a situation would bring, empty shelves in our food shops and, as a consequence, an inevitable hike in food prices!

Hopefully, by the time this book goes to print all the uncertainty over the European Union will have been resolved and Snowbird Foods, along with the raft of other UK profitable manufacturers will be allowed, once more, to contribute to Britain's economic future and job creation.

References

Paul, Philip (joint Managing Director of Snowbird Foods), interview (February 2019)

SAINSBURY'S LEA VALLEY
DISTRIBUTION DEPOTS

In the mind of the general public, Sainsbury's is an established and respected name in the retail food and drink industry that has fed successive generations of Britons for as long as they can remember. Not a great deal is known about the founder, John James Sainsbury, apart from a brief entry in the 1870 edition of *Kelly's Post Office Street Directory* which lists him as "Sainsbury, John, Dairyman, 173 Drury Lane, Holborn, London". According to Bridget Williams, the author of the *Best Butter in the World, the History of Sainsbury's*, the foundation of the company is generally taken to be 20th April 1869, the day that John married Mary Ann Staples at the parish church of St Giles-in-the-Fields, Holborn. It would seem that Mary played a crucial part in John's early business venture as, during the first few years, she ran the Drury Lane shop.

150 years after the founding, Sainsbury's has become Britain's third largest food retailer boasting a portfolio of some 2,200 supermarkets and convenience stores across the UK and Ireland which also sell a range of clothing. These include the recently acquired Argos chain of companies which sell a vast range of general household merchandise.

In recent years Sainsbury's built an enormous warehouse on part of the former Royal Gunpowder Mills south site at Waltham Abbey in the mid Lea Valley. The warehouse was constructed close to the M25 London ring-road to allow easy access to Sainsbury's southern stores.

In a rapidly changing world, with many people choosing to purchase goods and services online, Sainsbury's, to support its 190,000 internet customers, has taken over an empty warehouse in the lower Lea Valley, at Bromley-by-Bow, to create a "dark store". The "dark store", provoked by the expansion of online shopping, is a relatively new concept that allows Sainsbury's to collate customer's orders for same-day delivery and also for customer collection. Members of the public are not allowed into the "dark store", but if they were, they would recognise the space laid out rather like a conventional supermarket with aisles, shelves and freezers containing all

Sainsbury's 'dark store' warehouse, Twelvetrees Business Park, Bromley-by-Bow, London (courtesy Sainsbury's)

Mike Cope, CEO Sainsbury's (courtesy Sainsbury's)

Sainsbury's Head Office, Holborn, London (courtesy Sainsbury's)

Sainsbury's distribution depot Waltham Abbey (courtesy Sainsbury's)

Sainsbury's first shop 173 Drury Lane, London (courtesy Sainsbury's)

the familiar foods. Pickers move along the aisles and fill wheelie baskets, much like a shopper, with customer's online orders which are then taken to home dispatch or customer collection bays.

From a single store in 1869, Sainsbury's 150-year food journey has certainly come a long way in supporting the changing shopping habits of the general public. However, there is clearly a high price to pay, as witnessed by the daily media coverage of our shrinking high streets with empty stores and charity shops, mainly due to the rapid expansion of internet shopping. The author is conscious of constantly being reminded that our jobs are being gradually eroded and being taken over by robots and this is, of course, a good thing as it will eventually allow us more leisure time to amuse and enjoy ourselves. With this happy thought in mind, and with all this extra leisure time to spare, which has been created by robots and online shopping, it is possible that some "bright spark" will come up with a fantastic new idea, like; ***how about inventing a high street where we can enjoy ourselves by spending our newly won leisure time by all going shopping and communicating and talking with real people instead of computer screens!***

References

Correspondence and discussions with Sainsbury's Press Office and also Archives Department (April 2019)

Williams, Bridget, *The Best Butter in the World – A History of Sainsbury's*, Ebury Press, London (1994)

TAZAKI FOODS, ENFIELD – ANOTHER LEA VALLEY INTERNATIONAL DISTRIBUTOR AND PROVISIONS IMPORTER

Post-war immigrants to the UK, particularly those from parts of the old British Empire, brought with them their food and cultures which have added new districts to our towns and cities with shops, restaurants and regular festivals that have helped regenerate often seriously rundown areas, making these places colourful attractions that we can all enjoy without having to leave Britain. In recent years we have also seen immigrants moving from Eastern European and Mediterranean countries to Britain to fill jobs, particularly within the National Health Service, agriculture and the service industries, and they in turn have encouraged ethnic food outlets to set up to serve their communities, many of these in long-term empty shops and premises that currently fill our failing high streets, bringing areas back to life. Of course, this has opened up further opportunities for entrepreneurs by increasing the demand for exotic food imports from abroad.

Following the austerity years after the post Second World War period, cautiously adventurous Britons began taking holiday trips to destinations overseas that would have been far beyond the means and the aspirations of their parents. This opened up introductions to a large range of unfamiliar foods which had tastes, flavours and smells that were completely different from some of our favourite staples, like the traditional Sunday roast, bacon butties, fish and chips with mushy peas, and of course the nice, but unhealthy, full English breakfast! However, as a corollary to this gastronomic adventure, many overseas destinations saw a money-making oppor-tunity and rapidly set up British-styled eateries and Public Houses solely to cater for the non-adventurous and un-gastronomic Brit who would never ever counte-nance "anything foreign", only eating "traditional English meals". Luckily for those non-adventurous Brits, many of these anglicised eateries have also latched on to another UK favourite and offer "chips with everything"! Interestingly, as the years progressed into the 21st century and the overseas tourist boom continued, savvy entrepreneurs introduced a range of new restaurants to their faraway paradise that offered, Indian, Chinese and Thai cuisine, that have now become an embedded part of the UK's takeaway culture! Now, those of us who spend our hard-earned cash on the annual trip abroad enjoy all the foodie delights just as we do at home, so what is not to like about our holiday overseas!

Eventually, British farmers and horticulturalists saw opportunities to introduce new fruits and vegetables into their growing plans and began planting crops like capsi-cums, aubergines, chillies and sweet potatoes that, apart from giving the consumer a cost-effective choice, have helped to lower the UK's carbon footprint by reducing the miles these foods would normally have to travel from abroad. New nurseries and packhouses have been built or extended by the British growers to cope with this upsurge in business, which in turn has created jobs.

Over the years, as overseas travel increased, many British palates developed cosmo-politan tastes and this has led to the setting up of a range of restaurants and take-aways that cater for the UK's new-found dietary requirements gained with the help of the holiday abroad experience. Many home-cooked meals have now taken on a new lease of life with amateur chefs producing a veritable range of curries, pastas and stir-fry dishes. This has helped to introduce these new tastes and flavours to a wider circle of family members which has completely changed the way many of us shop, in an effort to satisfy the constantly evolving British diet.

These evolving trends have been picked up by grocery shops and supermarkets that have latched on to this growing food revolution and are now stocking strange and exotic ingredients. Many of these ingredients had previously been unheard of. Now shoppers can cater for their families' newly-found craving for a variety of internationally devised dishes. No longer can Britain be accused, by countries abroad, of only providing uninteresting food.

A visitor to the grocer or supermarket today can be overwhelmed by the large range of sauces, spices, fruit, vegetables (many out of season) and ready-meals on offer, most of these aimed at the home dinner party and the quick-and-easy microwave market. These changes in our eating habits and lifestyles has resulted in a high number of specialist wholesalers setting up in Britain to import and distribute foodstuffs to the rapidly expanding UK market. The outcome of this has been the creation of a massive logistics network of warehouses, cold stores and accompanying transport in support of this food-driven trend.

One of the popular sushi products carried by Tazaki Foods

Media companies saw new opportunities waiting to be exploited. Now cookery books fill the shelves of our bookshops and libraries and almost every day we seem to have wall-to-wall cooking programmes filling our television screens, often presented by the chefs and cooks that have authored this profusion of cookery books.

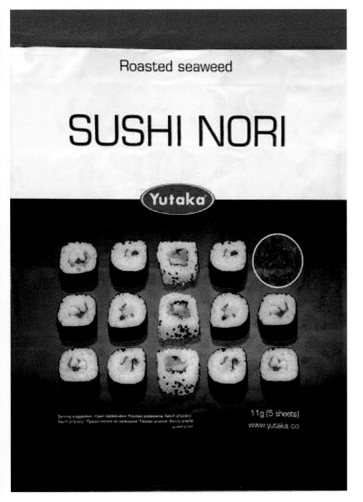

In 1978, Tazaki Foods an importer of traditional Japanese food and drink products, moved into a 69,000 square foot distribution centre on the Innova Park, Enfield to supply the UK's growing sushi bar and restaurant trade. And with the popularity of these new Asian tastes spreading, British supermarkets soon began receiving requests from their customers for more new and exotic ingredients. As the taste for Japanese cuisine grew, the Tazaki Foods business decided to expand its operation to distribute its products into Europe and beyond.

The date 1978 for the founding of Tazaki Foods in the UK is probably no coincidence as the timing follows two significant events that considerably affected Japanese manufacturing interests in Britain. In 1967 the British Broadcasting Corporation (BBC) began the first public service broadcasts of colour television in the UK using the German 625-line PAL system. In 1973, Britain joined the European Common Market. This gave Japanese manufacturers of television receivers like Sony, Hitachi and Toshiba the opportunity to set up factories in the UK, many in the manufacturing plants of former indigenous UK television companies. The strategic plan for these Japanese manufacturers was to produce television receivers and associated equipment in the UK, that

Tazaki Foods Innova Park, Enfield

Tazaki Foods warehouse, Innova Park, Enfield

would allow them to get under the European tariff barriers. Prior to this, Japanese companies had to pay substantial import duties. Also, television receivers imported from Japan were limited to screen sizes of no more than 13 inches.

The Japanese automotive industry also took advantage of Britain joining the European Common Market and major Japanese car manufacturers like Honda, Toyota and Nissan established factories in the UK to take advantage of Britain's market membership, giving them vast tax advantages and allowing the Japanese to competitively price their vehicles. While these new electronic and automotive factories created many jobs for British workers and also helped fill the coffers of the exchequer, these manufacturers brought managers and engineers from the home country to help setup and run the new production and design facilities. Naturally, the Japanese workforce were not accustomed to the foods that were on offer to the average Briton and craved the nourishment of traditional food and cooking ingredients from their homeland. This provided opportunities for the embryonic Tazaki Foods and also encouraged the restaurant sector in Britain to become more diverse. Tazaki Foods has now become a leading importer and wholesaler of traditional Japanese foods, supplying over 2,000 different product lines to major supermarket chains and restaurants across Europe.

References
Conversations and correspondence with representatives of Tazaki Foods
(December 2018)

Note

In this chapter we have seen how leading Japanese distributers and manufacturers chose to set up in Britain to take advantage of the UK's membership of the European Union allowing them to take advantage of the low tariff exports and imports with Europe. This has injected considerable wealth into the British economy and created jobs.

On June 5th 1975, the British electorate expressed support, in a referendum, for continuing membership of the European Common Market with 67 per cent in favour. The national turnout was 64 per cent of the registered voters. On 23rd June 2016, the British electorate voted, in a referendum, 51.9 per cent leave and 48.1 per cent remain. The national turnout was 72.2 per cent of the registered voters, (figures obtained from The Electoral Commission)

Several establishments, visited by the author, have expressed concerns with regard to government indecision over the Brexit issue, as they are unable to make long-term investment plans. Hopefully, the matter will be resolved in the very near future to give the Lea Valley businesses the outcome they desire to keep investing in the region.

BEAVERTOWN BREWERY – WHAT'S IN A NAME?

"Beavertown" is said to have got its name from local Cockneys who had mispronounced the area of "De Beauvoir Town", a part of Haggerston, Hackney, North London, the region in which the Beavertown Brewery was originally founded.

In 2011 Beavertown Brewery was founded by Logan Plant, the son of Lead Zeppelin's frontman Robert Plant. In an interview with *The Guardian* that documented his early life, Logan explained that when he was growing up in the West Midlands he was, "dragged around many of the old pubs of the Black Country by my dad. Eventually, I fell in love with the beer. At 20, I had a dream of opening a brewery somewhere in the middle of nowhere. I put that on the back burner and went into the music industry for about 10 years".

When touring in America as the frontman for the rock band, Sons of Albion, Logan was introduced to US craft beer and he discovered that it complemented some of his favourite barbecue foods. This was probably Logan's "Eureka" moment that gave him the idea of creating a brew pub. Logan's earlier association with beer, inherited from his trips with his father, had also made him curious about how the beverage was brewed and he took every opportunity to read up on the subject, amassing a large collection of specialist books. Also, when touring in America he visited various breweries and picked the brains of the owners and the brewers who seemed willing to share their creative passions.

On leaving the band, Logan, who freely admits to having no previous business experience, decided to live his dream. However, without having the necessary capital to fund his brewing passion, he first had to go through a difficult and painful period of trying to secure a loan from the banks. Naturally, as one might expect, these establishments were not particularly keen on funding a young man without any track record in business whatsoever. Eventually, he did discover one bank who

Artist's impression of Beaverworld, Enfield

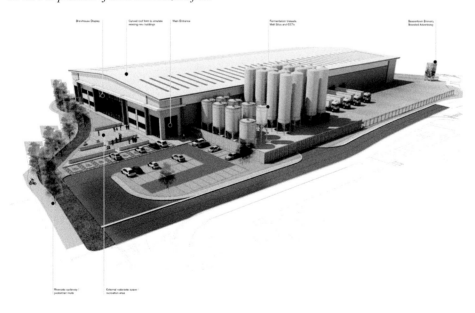

Contractors' equipment clearing former Ediswan site to allow building of Beavertown Brewery

were prepared to take the risk and funding was secured. Now, Logan could put his brewing interests into motion. This he did in the kitchen of his London home with a set of rather unconventional brewing apparatus, consisting of a 50-litre rice pan as a hot liquor tank, a picnic cool box as a mash tun and a tea urn as a kettle. Logan experimented, developed and perfected his craft-brewing techniques, although he admitted the process made his home rather smelly!

In 2011, now satisfied that he had acquired a reasonable level of brewing skills, Logan established his new business at 33 Downham Road, London N1and named it Duke's Brew & Que. Now the moment had arrived when this entrepreneurial brewer could begin living his dream with a microbrewery that had the capacity to produce around 650 litres of very palatable brews, which Logan's embryonic customer base seemed to enjoy. When asked by Holly O'Mahony, a reporter for *The Guardian*, "What's been your proudest moment"? Logan replied, "Serving the first batch of beer that I brewed at Duke's. Seeing people enjoy something you've made, in an environment you've constructed, is amazing."

New Beavertown Brewery, Enfield under construction, July 2019

New Beavertown Brewery starts to take shape

In a relatively short period of time, Duke's Brew & Que became a popular destination and a faithful clientele built up who were enjoying the experience of the new range of quirkily named craft beers on offer along with the variety of American-style barbecued foods. By 2013, Duke's, had become the platform for launching Logan's craft beers like Neck Oil (the recipe coming from Logan's memories of his favourite West Midlands Best Bitter) Smog Rocket, a Smoked Porter and 8 Ball Rye IPA, to a wider audience, and appears to have whetted the palates of a growing number of customers and beer enthusiasts. In fact, the beers had become so popular that demand for the Beavertown beverage began to outstrip the brewing capacity at the Downham Road site.

Now Logan and his team had reached a critical point in the development of the business, and the big question loomed, "shall we stay as we are or should we expand". Fortunately, the question had already been partially answered as from the start, the decision had been made to plough profits back into the operation and that allowed Logan the initial amount of capital to secure a 2,500 square foot production site; Unit 4, Stour Road, Hackney Wick. When this property was acquired, there was considerable pressure for a rapid transfer of the brewing equipment to the new site to help keep production flowing so customers would not be disappointed. A small team of six of Logan's faithful workers spent just one week preparing the Hackney Wick building, digging trenches, installing electrics, modifying plumbing, painting walls and levelling floors, while at the same time installing the brewing equipment. These tasks would probably not have been achieved in such a short time frame if outside contractors had been employed to do the work.

As more craft beers with popular new flavours were added to the Beavertown range, demand, rapidly began to outstrip the production capacity at the Hackney Wick brewery and by 2014 Logan's team were on the lookout for a larger production site, within the London region, with improved road access. Two suitable adjacent units of 5,500 square feet each were eventually found that fitted the requirements at Tottenham Hale. This, for the first time, allowed the brewing operation to be separated from the storage of the dry ingredients and packaged beer that was awaiting delivery. Within a year of the move, new brewing equipment had to be installed to, yet again, massively increase capacity as the unrelenting demand for Beavertown's craft beers gathered pace. Part of this was probably due to Logan's marketing strategy

The old Ediswan building before partial demolition to make way for Beavertown Brewery

that heavily relied on the colourful and quirky labelling of his canned beers. The creator of these somewhat psychedelic designs was Nick Dwyer. Nick was formerly a waiter at Dukes who had an artistic flare and had begun creating labelling concepts in his spare time. Logan was so impressed with Nick's work that he was made Beavertown's Creative Director.

From a kitchen brewery, in just three-and-a-half years, Beavertown's brewing output, at Tottenham Hale, was now (2015) almost ten times higher than that at Duke's. Moreover, Logan was exporting his products to at least 20 different countries; suggesting that the new flavours of his craft beers had taken on an international following that was continuing to grow.

On the 8th December 2017, the *Hackney Citizen*, ran the headline, "**Beavertown Brewery's sudden decision to axe former Hackney home Duke's Brew & Que leaves drinkers stunned**." The article went on to say, "The shock decision to shutter (sic) the brewpub and barbecue joint was announced in a statement released 4 December, signed by Logan Plant (Beavertown co-founder and son of Led Zeppelin singer Robert) and Team Beaver." The sudden closure of Dukes was met with sadness by many of the brewpub's fans, some took to social media to express their feelings of not being able to say farewell to the staff who had become friends of the regulars. However, it would appear that Logan and his team had been considering closure of Duke's Brew & Que for some time and the author suspects that the barbecue restaurant side of the business did not make a good commercial fit with Beavertown Brewery's long-term expansion strategy.

It would appear that the author's thoughts carried some validity as it would soon be announced that Beavertown Brewery had sold a minor share in the company to the Dutch brewing giant Heineken for £40 million. When the news of the deal broke some of Beavertown's customers refused to trade with the brewer as they believed the arrangement would mean that the company was no longer independent. However, as clarified in a recent Beavertown newsletter, Logan explained; "We retain full control of our destiny. I continue to be the founder, CEO and visionary leading the Beavertown charge and the people that you deal with here at the brewery are and will continue to be the dedicated Team Beaver. Heineken want to support us where we want it and otherwise leave us to get on with what we do best. If there is anything they can help with to improve the business across the board, they are there to assist, if we reach out. Beavertown will be the same as we always were, and we will continue to forge our own path together as Team Beaver. We retain the freedom to do our own thing."

James Dewar

From a person that had openly admitted that he had no previous business experience, Logan certainly appears to have learned many new commercial skills in a very short time! Logan, with his dedicated team, had brought his business to a point where his dream of building a global brand for the brewery had reached a climax and the Heineken investment would allow him the opportunity to do just that. In 2018 land clearance began at the site of the old Ediswan lamp works in Duck Lees Lane, Ponders End, in preparation for Logan's dream, with the construction of his new brewery; to be called Beaverworld. It is estimated that the new brewery will be up and running by the end of 2019. Also, it is planned to keep the Tottenham Hale site fully operational to help cope with the projected demand for craft beers.

It has been a pleasure to track the progress of Logan Plant on his journey that followed his dreams. All he has achieved has been through hard work and personal sacrifice. He recognised the need to build a dedicated likeminded team with the vision and dedication to succeed. However, the author would like to take the opportunity once more to remind all those who think they have found the perfect business formula to fame and fortune; ***when you believe your business is most successful, that is when your business is most vulnerable***.

Those readers who are familiar with the author's background as an electronics engineer, will no doubt recall the many times that he has claimed in lectures and broadcasts that the Ediswan, Ponders End site, where Logan is building his new brewery, has now become known as "The Centre of the Universe" because of its technological importance.

In keeping with the theme of this book which highlights, where possible, the history and backstories of the various Lea Valley food and drink sites, the reader might like to refer to the article, originally published in the *EN Magazine*, April 2018, in the footnote to this chapter.

References

Barnes, Andrew, *Beavertown Brewery's sudden decision to axe former Hackney home Duke's Brew & Que leaves drinkers stunned*, Hackney Citizen, 8th December, 2017

O'Mahony, Holly, *Logan Plant: going on the road with my dad opened my eyes*, The Guardian, 13th June, 2017

Sigee, Rachael, *Hop idol: how Robert Plant's son Logan is riding the new craft beer wave with Beavertown Brewery*. Evening Standard, 28th October, 2015

PART OF THE CENTRE OF THE UNIVERSE GOES MISSING!

Joseph Wilson Swan

Professor Ambrose Fleming

The Duck Lees Lane plaque

As an electronics engineer, who once worked for the former Thorn EMI Ferguson company, I have a unique claim to fame. That of proclaiming that Duck Lees Lane, Ponders End, Enfield is the centre of the universe! To a certain extent the Institute of Physics supported this notion by sponsoring a plaque that was erected on site in 2009 and unveiled by the Mayor of Enfield. Recently it was reported by a senior council officer that the plaque, which had been installed on a building around six metres above ground level, has gone missing. Why am I so concerned about the loss and why have I made, what appears to be, such an outlandish claim?

In 1886, Joseph Wilson Swan (1828-1914) (later Sir) moved his lamp factory from South Benwell in north-east England to a site beside the River Lea at Ponders End, Enfield. Although Swan had demonstrated a crude form of electric lamp almost 20 years before the American Thomas Alva Edison had registered his own version, he had failed to patent the device. Swan had naively believed that the technology he had used was already in the public domain and well understood. Rather than fight an expensive legal battle in the courts over the invention Swan joined with Edison and the Ediswan Company (as it eventually became known) was formed.

John Ambrose Fleming (1849-1945), a prominent scientist, was invited to join the company as a consultant to investigate the blackening on the inside of light bulbs, resulting from the "Edison effect". This had been primarily caused, in Swan's case, by carbon deposits released from his unique cellulosed thread filaments. Fleming had the Ponders End laboratory make a number of lamps with an extra electrode (anode) on which he carried out his experiments.

After completing his work, Fleming took an extra consultancy with the Marconi Wireless Telegraph Company. Being involved with Marconi may have given him the idea of improving the method for the detection of radio waves. Until then, the favoured device for detection was the coherer, an insulated tube filled with loose iron particles which conducted when a signal was applied. The device had the distinct disadvantage of having to be gently tapped after each operation to free the particles ready for the next signal.

In 1904, Fleming registered an improved version of his earlier experimental device, the world's first thermionic valve, a diode, (two electrode) British Patent No. 24850. The term "valve" was borrowed from mechanical nomenclature and implies a means of control. In the electronic sense, the diode valve controls the passage of an oscillating radio wave by allowing it to pass in only one direction. This is the method of detection which, after suitable processing allows our radio receivers, to convert the radio signals which have been transmitted from the numerous broadcast stations around the world into intelligible speech and music.

It was perhaps fitting that the patenting of Fleming's device had, in a way, made up for Edison claiming the invention of the electric lamp ahead of Swan. Edison himself, in the early 1880s, had concluded that the blackening on the inside of the light bulb was caused by electrically charged particles of carbon flowing as a current stream from the filament. He had also concluded that the current in the bulb varied with the temperature of the filament. This, he observed, was directly related to the supply voltage. Apart from constructing an "electrical indicator" as a result of his experiments, it would appear that Edison had not attached any other commercial value to his discovery.

However, it was Fleming's understanding, and his commercial grasp, of the importance of Edison's discoveries regarding the electron emissions as current flow from a heated filament which allowed him to seize a missed opportunity which he exploited.

Appreciating what Edison had missed, and also understanding the requirements for the detection of an oscillating wave, Fleming was uniquely positioned to make the discovery of the century. With the modified light bulbs from Ponders End, Fleming was able to bring together, for the first time, the technology of the lamp and the electronic control of a wireless signal. With the extra electrode (anode) the electric lamp had effectively become the diode valve.

In a way, Fleming's discovery might be considered an act of fate, or perhaps natural justice, as he had made up for Swan's slowness in registering his invention before the American.

It can be claimed, on the basis of Fleming's work on Swan's electric lamp that the post-industrial revolution – the technological revolution – began at Ponders End, Enfield. The diode valve was only one of many exciting industrial firsts for the Lea Valley region. From this simple beginning has grown the multimedia communications industry of today and the way has been paved for even more exciting technological developments in industry, entertainment and leisure. When the Olympics came to the lower Lea Valley, in 2012, it was the embryonic technology, developed in Duck Lees Lane, Ponders Enfield that allowed the athletic events to be beamed live around world as they happened for everyone to see.

At the present rate of electronic progress, it is almost impossible to imagine the rapid growth of communications technology 114 years after Fleming's patent. Even Swan himself, who had pioneered and witnessed many remarkable scientific achievements, which, for the day, would have probably seemed equally unimaginable, could not have dreamed of how far we have come.

While writing this piece I have been informed that the plaque is in safe keeping. Apparently, it was taken down and stored by a conscientious site developer and will be reinstated when building work is completed. Now residents of Enfield can relax and feel justly proud that Duck Lees Lane will once again return to the centre of the universe, the only place on our planet where the post-industrial, the technological revolution, began!

Restored façade of Ediswan building with plaque reinstated, July 2019. A reminder to future generations where the centre of the universe resides!

A production Ediswan diode valve c1906 with a bayonet cap (BC) base

References

Lewis, Jim, *London's Lea Valley Britain's Best Kept Secret,* Phillimore & Co. Ltd, Chichester (1999)

Lewis, Jim, 'Part of the Centre of the Universe Goes Missing!', *EM Journal* (May 2018)

Note

In July 2019 the author visited the Duck Lees Lane site at Ponders End and was astonished to see that the façade of the Ediswan building had been tastefully preserved and painted. Also, the plaque had been reinstated to its original position. Therefore, the author would like to say a big thank you to Logan Plant and his team for restoring the "Centre of the Universe"!

A BUILDING SHARED BY TWO WHOLESALE ASIAN FOOD SUPPLIERS HAS A UNIQUE BACKSTORY!

In different parts of a "recycled" factory building in rundown Lockfield Avenue, Brimsdown, Enfield, two Asian food wholesalers have set up successful businesses. No longer do Chinese and Indian restaurants have to deal directly with suppliers in the Far East for their spices, herbs, general ingredients and utensils, as just an email, text or phone call to two of Enfield's Asian specialists, Hoo Hing and Dacca Caterers, will ensure delivery of the order. The growing popularity of Asian, West Indian, Italian, Japanese, Turkish, Greek and other foods with the British public, has created a massive supply chain infrastructure cluster within the Lea Valley region. Now many busy people seem to be losing the art of cooking as it is now a simple matter to satisfy hunger pangs with takeaways, fast-food emporiums, home delivered meals and eating out. All these services appear to be on the increase.

The "unique backstory", mentioned in this chapter's heading, is about a modern-day Lea Valley hero who, in the 1960s, had held a position of considerable importance, in a new building in Lockfield Road, that is currently occupied by Hoo Hing and Dacca Caterers. The author would be very surprised if the present owners of these two businesses have any knowledge of the history of their current workspace.

Vincent Emmanuel Campbell, Vince to his friends, was born in the remote southern part of Jamaica on 28th September 1928. His father worked as a sugar refiner for the giant Tate & Lyle Company while his mother ran a dressmaking and catering business. Vince's schooling was not untypical for a West Indian child from such a background. After attending junior school his Christian parents sent him to a boarding school, away from the district, where discipline was strict. He was also encouraged, by his parents, to attend the local Anglican Church three to four times on a Sunday and this he did until the age of 15.

Alencoflex products designed to accommodate a range of different industrial applications

A range of Oriental food products on display at Hoo Hing, Brimsdown, Enfield

Between 15 and 16 Vince received private tuition before taking examinations that were similar to the British General Certificate of Education. When his schooling was completed Vince began a five-year engineering apprenticeship with Tate & Lyle. After two years of training, at the age of 18, he felt the need for a greater challenge. Not sure quite what he wanted he thought he would try the British Army, but before he could be accepted, he had to take an entrance exam, which he easily passed. Two years into army life and Vince was again becoming restless so he decided to return to Tate & Lyle to complete his interrupted apprenticeship. However, his short army career had not been totally wasted for it was during this time that he met the woman who was to become his wife and life-long partner.

EⁱⁱR

The Master of the Household
has received Her Majesty's command to invite

Mr. V. E. Campbell

to a Reception to be given at Buckingham Palace
by The Queen and The Duke of Edinburgh
for Holders of The Queen's Award to Industry
on Tuesday, 10th February, 1976 at 6 p.m.

An invitation from the Queen and the Duke of Edinburgh to Vince Campbell to attend a reception at Buckingham Palace

After Vince had served his apprenticeship his restless nature once again led him to seek greater challenges and, although Tate & Lyle had promoted him to an executive position, he was unable to suppress his inner drive to achieve something else. In 1954, like many of his countrymen and women, he left his beloved homeland and came to Britain, still driven by this urge to achieve, as yet, some unidentified goal. He arrived late one cold October night in Tottenham where he had planned to stay with a friend until he found work. Unfortunately, due to a number of unplanned circumstances, his friend was unable to offer accommodation. Cold and disillusioned, Vince was convinced that he had made the biggest mistake of his life by coming to such an inhospitable country. Fortunately, Vince found temporary accommodation in Tottenham and after a short unhappy existence where he took on any type of menial work, he eventually plucked up courage to write to his father to borrow money for the return fare home, only to be told that he must stick it out. No doubt his strict West Indian father had thought his son was being too hasty. Eventually, through a contact at his local Anglican Church, his luck improved and a job offer came from a member of the congregation who had clearly recognised the potential in this young man.

Dacca Indian foods, Brimsdown, Enfield

Hoo Hing warehouse and supermarket, Brimsdown, Enfield

Inside Dacca Indian foods warehouse

The works and offices of Alenco Hilyn in Lockfield Avenue, Brimsdown c1970, the building now occupied by Dacca Foods and Hoo Hing

Vince found lodgings (bed and breakfast at £2-50 a week) at Amhurst Road, Stamford Hill with a Mrs King. There he set about the serious task of improving his educational skills by taking correspondence courses with an establishment based in Manchester. During this period Vince was able to gain a considerable amount of experience, which would later be of great value, by working at a number of jobs in tool making and general engineering. However, his insatiable drive to achieve something better had once more come to the fore. Seeing a newspaper advertisement, he applied for, and got, a job with Cyril Austin, an engineering design agency located at Bishopsgate, in London's East End. Here Vince put his engineering knowledge to practical use when he became involved with the design and development of industrial high-pressure hoses. Vince soon became accepted as a valued member of the team and it was not long before it was decided that the company should move into the manufacture of hoses and associated products. At the beginning this was achieved by making products with the material, polytetrafluoroethylene (PTFE), sourced from Germany. The giant multinational companies ICI and Dupont were the main suppliers of this material, which was also used in the manufacture of thread seal tape.

Soon it became clear that the increasing volume of business was too great for the cramped Bishopsgate premises and in 1957 the company moved to a larger building in Lockfield Avenue Brimsdown in the London borough of Enfield. Vince recalls that, at the time, Brimsdown was a pretty inhospitable place, particularly in winter, when fog and mists from the River Lea enveloped the area and always seemed to be present. However, it would appear that the hostile environment only acted as a spur to Vince who was once more looking to satisfy his driving urge to achieve. At the new plant he had expected to be given greater responsibilities as recognition for all his hard work and dedication in promoting good engineering practice. Although the company was prospering and had started taking on new staff, Vince was not offered the responsibility that he felt he had earned so he decided to leave. Fortunately, he was persuaded to stay and, as it will later become clear, he had obviously made his point.

Soon the company had outgrown the Lockfield Avenue site and, with a government grant, moved to new purpose-built premises erected a little distance along the road.

Vince Campbell with work colleagues after returning from Buckingham Palace with the Queens Award to Industry

Vince Campbell with work colleagues before setting off to Buckingham Palace to receive the Queen's Award to Industry from Her Majesty

Now, as the newly promoted Works Manager, Vince took on more staff and created an evening shift, which proved popular, as it provided much needed work for local women. The reputation of the company, as a quality manufacturer of high-pressure hoses and associated products, was becoming known internationally and to cope with the growing order book new production processes had to be found. At the time, it was thought, by many in the plastics industry, that PTFE could not be success-fully used to manufacture products in large quantities. However, it would seem that the industry pundits had not heard of the tenacious Vince Campbell. Working in secret with his team, day and night for a year, Vince perfected a manufacturing process that allowed the company to become one of the largest producers of their kind in Europe, if not the world. The measure of the success of the new process can be gauged by the company achieving the prestigious approval, for its products, of the UK Ministry of Defence. Leading companies with household names, such as British Oxygen, British Gas, Volvo, General Electric and a host of others also gave their approval, after first subjecting the process to the close scrutiny of their experts.

With the high cost of developing the new process an injection of capital was needed and the decision was taken to sell the company, now known as Alenco Hilyn Limited, to the Charterhouse Group. At the time, Charterhouse were a £150 million publicly-quoted company based in the City of London with merchant banking and industrial interests. Therefore, it had been reasoned that the necessary cash would be provided to guarantee that the highest quality production standards could be maintained over the long term.

At the age of 49, Vince achieved what the cold and unhappy West Indian young man, in 1954, could never have imagined, the appointment to the Board of his company as Managing Director, with the added responsibility for international trouble-shooting. It would now seem that Vince had found the hidden reason for his insatiable drive, but perhaps not, was there more to come? In his new position Vince travelled the world, not only solving technical problems, but also as a respected ambassador and a role model for the black community, showing young people what could be achieved through hard work, dedication and vision.

On Tuesday 10th February1976, Vince received the ultimate honour when he was invited to Buckingham Palace to receive the Queen's Award to Industry from Her Majesty, the first black Managing Director to be so rewarded. This, as one might imagine was a proud moment for Vince. However, in his heart the award was not just accepted on behalf of his company, but also as recognition for the worth of the black community and other ethnic minorities, who, at the time were grossly under-represented in supervisory jobs in industry and commerce.

During Vince's time within industry his life had not only been taken up with company matters and the goals of self-achievement, he was also committed passionately to promoting equal opportunities for the black community and other ethnic minority groups. He explained to the author that he wanted black people to be treated as equals within our society, not just tolerated. Vince understood the problems of racial discrimination well, even as a senior manager he was not personally free from incident. In both his private and industrial life, he had experienced many examples of racial abuse. Once, when visiting Carolina in the United States of America, Vince, along with a number of senior managers from Europe, had been invited by the President of a large company to a breakfast meeting at his home. On arrival, Vince was singled out and asked what he was doing there. When he explained that his name was Vince Campbell and he had been invited to take breakfast with the President he was allowed into the meeting. When relating the incident to the author some years later, Vince explained, with a laugh, that he had received the invitation because, through his Celtic name, they had thought he was Scottish. He then went on to say that when the maid, who was serving the beverage, entered the room and saw him, she nearly dropped the coffee jug. There were many such incidents as these, in all parts of the world, during Vince's time as Managing Director.

In 1976, due to his public-spirited commitment, Vince became Chairman of the Enfield Community Relations Council (CRC) and was instrumental in setting up a number of support agencies for the under privileged. Fortunately, his company was sympathetic to his civic duties, recognising the worth of his community work. Vince was allowed three days off a month to attend meetings and to continue the momentous task of setting up the necessary early support structures to achieve this goal. This he did by lobbying Councillors, Members of Parliament and Cabinet Ministers, in fact, anyone he could get to listen.

However, Vince's high community profile soon attracted the attention of several extremist individuals and groups. He began to receive hate mail, racist phone calls and even his life and that of his family was threatened when a bullet was fired through the window of his home. Needless to say, even these serious incidents could not shake the determination or the courage of this remarkable man.

On returning from a business trip to America in 1982, Vince was to learn that Charterhouse had taken the decision to get out of manufacturing and concentrate on its core business interests (in the financial sector) and he was made redundant. Now at the age of 54, he reasoned that it was unlikely that he would find a similar senior position in industry, so a change of strategy was required. He took the decision that he would work for himself and acquired two general stores in Waltham Forest. This new venture graphically demonstrated the difficulties of dealing with banks and other agencies, particularly if you were black, when lacking the necessary skills and experience. However, as might be imagined, this only acted as an added spur to Vince as he quickly realised that the problems that he had encountered, would also be experienced by others from the ethnic minority community who wished to set up on their own account. The encounter with the world of starting your own business resulted in the formation, in 1987, of the Black Business Association (BBA) and, with Vince as its Chairman, it helped many people to achieve their full potential as we progress into the new millennium.

It would take a whole book to record the achievements of this remarkable man who, through his sheer courage and determination has improved the lives of countless local people and, for the author, he will always remain a true Lea Valley hero.

References

Campbell, Vincent Emmanuel, interview (April 2000)
Correspondence with the "Enfield Revealed" project (April 2000)

BOOKER, MAKRO, ICELAND AND TESCO – WHAT ARE THE CONNECTIONS?

When researching the history of the Booker Group plc for this particular chapter, the author became entangled in a web of company names that initially caused considerable confusion with regard to who actually owned who and who are the companies that we buy our groceries from. In the piece that follows it will hopefully become a little clearer as we unpick the merger and takeover story.

The name "Booker" will be familiar with many readers who will associate it with the coveted Booker Prize for literature, but will not normally associate the name with the multi-billion food and drink industry. However, the name originally had no connection with the wholesale food and drink industry or with literature.

In 1835, John and Richard Booker established the Booker Line when they purchased their first ship. Originally the company specialised in transporting goods and later became involved with their distribution which showed improved profit margins. So much so that the shipping fleet was gradually sold off and the new business plan was to concentrate on wholesale food distribution. By 1978 the company owned over 100 food distribution warehouses across the UK and was trading as Booker McConnell Limited.

In the meantime, Booker had become involved in the sugar trade in the former colony of British Guiana. This eventually led them to take control of some 70 per cent of that country's sugar industry. Bookers, like many companies and private individuals, became powerful from the profits of sugar and it is sad to think that prosperity was achieved by exploiting the indigenous workforce. It was not until 1952, when the Fabian socialist, Jock Campbell, took over as chairman of the company that schemes were introduced that dramatically transformed the working conditions of the employees. Campbell is also responsible for creating Booker's Author Division, the sponsor of the Booker Prize.

A typical Booker wholesale depot (courtesy Booker)

Iceland warehouse, Solar Way, Enfield

In 1996, Booker purchased the food wholesale giant, Nurdin & Peacock, a company originally founded by Paul Agustin Nurdin after he arrived in Britain from France in 1810. Initially Nurdin's business was involved in the sale of eggs and dairy products. However, by the 1950s the company had grown into a massive wholesaler of general grocery products and had become one of the early pioneers of the cash and carry business model. By the year 2000, Booker's avid takeover programme took a temporary pause when it merged with the Iceland Supermarket chain, a company founded in 1970 by Malcolm Walker with business partner Peter Hinchliffe who were formerly employed by Woolworths.

In 2002, the Iceland-Booker holding company was renamed the Big Food Group (BFG) which in 2005 was bought by the Islandic retail consortium Baugur Group. Baugur split BFG into two separate companies, Icelandic retail and Booker Cash & Carry plc. In 2008, just prior to the Icelandic financial crisis, Baugur sold all its assets in Booker Cash & Carry. Then in February 2009, Baugur collapsed and its 77 per cent stake in Iceland Supermarkets fell into the ownership of Icelandic banks.

Inside the Makro warehouse, Enfield

In 2012 a consortium, which included the former founder of Iceland Supermarkets, Malcom Walker, purchased the Iceland stake from the Icelandic banks. Also, in 2012, Iceland acquired one of its food suppliers, Loxton Foods, and renamed the company Iceland Manufacturing Limited.

Prior to its collapse in 2009, Baugur had sold off all its assets in Booker Cash & Carry and the company was free to operate on its own account. In 2012 the Metro Group, that had previously bought the Makro stores in Europe from SHV Holdings, sold 30 of its stores in the UK complete with assets, to Booker Cash & Carry, making Booker one of the largest food wholesalers in Britain. The merger was referred to the Office of Fair Trading by the Competition Commission the deal being cleared in 2013.

Part of the Tesco Shire Park complex, Welwyn Garden City

The Makro warehouse, Stockingswater Lane, Enfield

By 2015, Booker had bought the Budgens and Londis grocery chains from the Musgrove Group for £40 million. Only two years later in, January 2017, the food retail giant Tesco announced that it had agreed a £3.7 billion merger with Booker Group. The group is now made up of several divisions which specialise in different areas of the UK wholesale food market which also includes supplying Premier, the nationwide independent convenient stores.

By now, no doubt the reader will be wondering do I have a choice of where my food comes from, or perhaps it's a question of as long as it remains relatively cheap does it really matter?

References

Author unknown, 'Booker Cash & Carry Ltd History', *International Directory of Company Histories, Vol.68.* St James Press (2005)

Author unknown, 'Booker swoops to buy up beleaguered Makro', *The Grocer* (May 2012)

Butler, Sarah, 'Iceland government challenges retail chain Iceland over name use', *The Guardian* (24th November 2016)

Walker, Malcom, *Best Served cold: The Rise and Fall and Rise Again of Malcolm Walker,* Icon Books (May 2014)

CAMDEN TOWN BREWERY – ANOTHER GREAT SUCCESS STORY

When researching the histories of the various successful breweries and microbreweries that have set up within the Lea Valley region the author discovered a common thread running through the investigation that binds them together. That thread is normally a single-minded individual with vision and passion is involved. In the case of Camden Town Brewery, the individual is Jasper Cuppaidge.

The maternal grandson of Laurie McLaughlin who ran McLaughlin's Brewery, along with a chain of some 60 public houses, in Rockhampton, Australia, from 1910 to 1960, one would have expected young Jasper to have taken a keen early interest in the industry. However, like many great success stories, Jasper's path which would eventually lead to fame and fortune took a very different, and more modest, route.

At the age of 20, in 1995, Jasper was actively living his passion for surfing and was determined to test the surf in several different countries. After sampling the waves in America, he left to try Africa, but missed his connecting flight to that continent from the UK. Needing to supplement his spending fund he got a job at *The Westbourne*, a public house in Notting Hill, West London where he became an ash tray cleaner and glass collector. Over a period of ten years, Jasper worked his way through the London public house hospitality industry, gaining considerable knowledge about the best and the worst attributes of the business. By 2006, with money that he had saved and with help from investors, Jasper was able to buy the *Horseshoe*, a rundown public house in Hampstead, North-West London. After renovation, and installation of a first-class chef, the *Horseshoe* soon started receiving good reviews from the food critics, but Jasper was not satisfied by the "wet" sales. In an interview with the *Kentishtowner*, Jasper explained; "Back then the native beer offering sucked – we imported American and European varieties but none from the UK. The local industry was flat, with no drive, ruled by CAMRA rather than creatively".

In 2007, in the basement of the *Horseshoes*, Jasper began his first brewing experiment making a batch of beer that he named Mac's in honour of his grandfather. Unfortunately, he was unable to use the name as the trademark was already owned.

Camden Town Brewery beer processing equipment, Navigation Park, Ponders End, Enfield

The new beer was an instant hit with the pub's customers and had also become popular with his pub-owner friends. Soon the small *Horseshoe* basement brewery was running out of capacity and Jasper was having to get his beer brewed in Europe to keep up with demand. Clearly, this was an unsatisfactory arrangement which required a radical rethink.

Jasper had spotted some nearby empty railway arches under Kentish Town West Station, and by mortgaging everything he owned up to the hilt, and also with investment from friends, he eventually managed to take over three arches. Interestingly, the year was 2008, the beginning of the financial recession, which meant the risk of Jasper's investment was high but because of the monetary crisis, the arches were relatively cheap as nobody wanted them.

Camden Town Brewery, Navigation Park, Ponders End, Enfield

Notice board Camden Town Brewery, Enfield – big enough not to miss

In the spring of 2010, what had become the Camden Town Brewery began brewing. Its first lager was called Hells which was a combination of Helles and Pilsner, brewed with hops and malt obtained from Germany. Jasper's idea was to ensure that his brewery made great beer and brand it so that it was easily identifiable by the consumer. The latter was achieved through Camden Town Brewery's logo of a castle, which refers to the four local Camden public houses, the Dublin, Edinboro, Pembroke and Windsor Castles.

Within five years of opening his brewery under the arches, Jasper's range of beers had increased exponentially and demand for his amber nectars had again gone through the roof. However, around 50 per cent of Camden's production was having to be farmed out to Belgium to help keep pace with demand. Now Jasper was faced, once again, with having to make, like many who had become rapidly successful before him, a momentous decision – "shall I remain or shall I expand". Finally, the decision was taken to build a brand-new brewery from scratch within the boundary of the London ring-road, the M25. A site, ten miles from Camden, at Ponders End, in the London Borough of Enfield was chosen for the project. Now, there was only one "slight" problem to solve, how to fund the project!

In early 2015 a crowdfunding campaign was begun which raised almost £3 million and then a big investor, Anheuser-Busch InBev, the world's largest brewer, reportedly came up with a further £10 million. Reading the various reports, the estimated cost of building the new Enfield brewery came in at around £30 million. Clearly there was a shortfall in funding for the project.

By December 2015 several media sources were reporting that AB InBev, which owns more than 500 brands, including Stella Artois, Budweiser and Becks (and in 2016 bought SAB Miller for £79 billion) had acquired Camden Town Brewery for £85 million. At the time the news of the buyout drew considerable criticism from the craft beer aficionados as they believed the control of AB InBev would compromise the individuality of quality and distinctive flavours that had become Camden's trademark. Rebutting this notion. Jasper Cuppaidge when interviewed by *The Guardian* explained; "AB InBev are investing to build a new brewery to our exact standards, so I can continue to make great beer. They're not making a beer for us". In a later *Guardian* interview Jasper was asked, if he would come under pressure to cut corners? Jasper replied; "I don't believe it will happen, we're a standalone business within the mothership". When speaking about a breakfast meeting with Carlos Brito, the CEO of AB InBev, Jasper said; "he was charming and we had a great conversation. The company has a winning culture. They are saying: Camden, keep doing what you do, and do it better, and if we can help you, we will".

In 2017 Jasper's new brewery opened in Enfield's Ponders End, making it the largest investment in London brewing for 30 years and also adding critical mass to the Lea Valley's growing food and drink industry.

References

Davies, Rob, 'Camden Town Brewery sold to world's biggest drinks company', *The Guardian* (21st December 2015)

Davies, Rob, 'Sale of Camden Town Brewery a sign of craft beer's fizzing into mainstream', *The Guardian* (23rd December 2015)

Emms, Stephen, 'The Story of Camden Town Brewery. And what's next?', *Kentishtowner* (8th November 2015)

Naylor, Tony, 'Has Camden Town Brewery ruined craft beer for everyone?', *The Guardian* (2nd January 2016)

Naylor, Tony, 'Why the pub isn't the only place that drinkers should buy craft beers', *The Guardian* (12th July 2017)

Robinson, Nicholas, 'Camden Town boss on criticism, investment and innovation', *The MA* (27th February 2017)

Smithers, Rebecca, 'British craft beer boom stalls as big drinks companies muscle in', *The Guardian* (23rd April 2019)

Wood, Zoe, 'Camden Town Brewery founder insists big can also be beautiful', *The Guardian* (8th July 2017)

Wood, Zoe, 'Craft beer makers hope to crack new markets with tap rooms', *The Guardian* (1st April 2018)

WANIS INTERNATIONAL FOODS – CATERING FOR WORLDWIDE PALATES

After World War Two, Britain welcomed new migrants from its Colonies across the world to fill job vacancies that had been created by the devastating effects of the recent conflict. These new settlers were required to rebuild Britain's National Health Service, get our transport systems moving and generally help the UK economy to get back on its feet. As one might imagine the new arrivals were unaccustomed to the vagaries of the British climate and many suffered during the long, cold, dark winter months. Also, at the time, Britain's grocery shops and street markets were still recovering from wartime shortages, with some foodstuffs still rationed, and of course it was not possible for the newcomers to buy the range of foods and spices that they were accustomed to in their different homelands. Many must have wondered what on earth they had done.

In 1964, Tulsidas Wadhwani (Mr Wani as he became known) left his native India and came to the UK and it was not long before he realised that there was a massive gap in Britain's grocery market. From Mr Wani's perspective it was clear that British retailers did not cater for the diverse range of foods that were normally cooked and enjoyed within the new ethnic minority communities that were beginning to become established, particularly those around London. Renting a small retail shop

Wanis International Foods, Leyton warehouse

Aisles at the Wanis International Foods, Leyton

Products on show at Wanis International Foods warehouse, Leyton

Wanis International Foods transport fleet

Stacked food aisles at Wanis International warehouse, Leyton

in Holloway Road, North London Mr Wani began importing several hard-to-obtain world foods like Jamaican Ackee and African Fufu Flour. Soon the word got around about the new shop that could source hard-to-find ethnic products and the customer base, along with range of foodstuffs stocked, quickly increased.

Over the coming years the business witnessed several moves into bigger premises and eventually transformed into a massive wholesale food operation. Progressing from originally supplying only the small ethnic London retailers, to supplying food businesses throughout the UK. These include leading supermarkets like the Co-op, Tesco, Sainsbury's, Asda, Waitrose and Morrisons as well as online retailers Amazon and Ocado.

Wanis International Foods, from its new 120,000 square foot purpose-built depot in Leyton, can claim to be Britain's largest wholesaler of some 10,000 ethnic food and drink products.

From a tiny shop in North London in 1964 the company, now with an annual turnover of £90 million, exports to over 28 countries across the world. Not bad from a one-man start-up business by an immigrant with exceptional vision!

References
Conversations and correspondence with Wanis International Foods marketing
    department, with particular thanks to Julian Davis

Wanis, artist's impression of Leyton warehouse

COCA-COLA – THE LEA VALLEY'S LARGEST NON-ALCOHOLIC DRINKS MANUFACTURER

Over the last few years the Lea Valley region has witnessed a steep rise in the establishment of craft beer brewhouses. The rise can be directly attributed to Gordon Brown when he was Chancellor of the Exchequer. In 2002 he introduced the Small Brewers' Relief Bill which substantially reduced excise duty for small brewers who were producing less than 60,000 hectoliters (10.56 million) pints per year. The system that Brown introduced works on a sliding scale, allowing larger tax breaks for smaller businesses. However, although the author has not worked out the mathematics it is reasonable to conclude that we consume more non-alcoholic beverages than those which are alcoholic.

In 1974, the arm of the world-famous drinks company, Coca-Cola European Partners, established a new production facility at Nobel Road, Edmonton in the London Borough of Enfield with a workforce of 229 employees.

Coca-Cola, or Coke as it is more commonly referred to, a carbonated soft drink, began life as a patent medicine. It was invented by John Stith Pemberton, a former Colonel in the Confederate Army who had been wounded in the American Civil War of 1861. Pemberton took morphine to relieve his pain from the wound and had become addicted to the drug. It is clear that he recognised his condition as he set out to find an alternative to the drug. In his effort to discover a substitute he set up Pemberton's Eagle Drug and Chemical House, a drugstore in Columbus, Georgia. Here Pemberton experimented and developed medicines which he sold in his drugstore by the glass alongside his soda-fountain drinks. These medicines he confidently claimed would cure a range of ailments from indigestion to impotence! One of these so-called medicines he had named Coca-Cola, which at the time, was made from coca leaves and the African kola nut, the latter added to give the mixture a caffeine boost. This combination of potent ingredients would have probably masked the patient's condition rather than actually curing it, allowing them to leave the drugstore with smiles on their faces and a feeling of pleasurable euphoria! No wonder the drink became so popular!

In the late 19th century, Pemberton sold his Coca-Cola formula to the businessman, Asa Griggs Chandler who used his marketing skills to heavily promote the product. Now the brand has become so well known that it ranks third in the world behind Apple and Google. It is claimed that the current Coca-Cola formula remains a

Coca-Cola new packaging plant, Enfield (courtesy Coca-Cola)

Coca-Cola plant, Eleys Estate, Enfield (courtesy Coca-Cola)   *Fuelling Coca-Cola vehicle with bio-gas (courtesy Coca-Cola)*

secret. However, with today's scientific knowhow and the many copycat brands in the marketplace, it is probable that someone has already come close to discovering the recipe!

Like many large multinational companies Coca-Cola wishes to present a caring public face, particularly regarding environmental issues, and to be fair, this notion is not just about creating an impressive public image, it also makes good economic sense too.

In 2012 Coca-Cola in the UK carried out a year-long trial that was organised in cooperation with Cenex, the government-funded Centre for Excellence. Two brand-new 26-ton Iveco Stralis lorries were bought, one fueled by diesel and one fueled by compressed biomethane gas. The object of the exercise was to discover if an overall reduction in dangerous CO_2 (carbon dioxide) and NOX (nitrogen oxides) emissions could be achieved across the whole Coca-Cola transport fleet. A temporary gas vehicle fueling plant was installed at the Enfield plant to assist the experiment. By the end of the year it was discovered that the gas fueled vehicle had dramatically reduced NOX and PM (particulate matter) emissions by 85.6 per cent and 97.1 per cent respectively, over its diesel competitor.

After the results of the trial, Darren O'Donnell, Coca-Cola's Logistics Asset Manager, announced; "Securing Cenex's involvement has given us the confidence to introduce new vehicle technology and fuels which will make step-changes in our emissions performance". At the time Coca-Cola purchased 13 additional new gas vehicles, making it the UK's largest CBM (compressed biomethane) fleet and immediately instituted plans to build a CBM fueling station at the Enfield plant. Incidentally, during these trials the biogas vehicle had a staggering availability rating of 99.2 per cent, making it more reliable and efficient than its diesel counterpart.

It would seem that Coco-Cola are taking the overall environmental issue very seriously as they recognise there is a clear efficiency and financial benefit to be had. The company were quick to spot the benefits of natural sunlight and installed solar panels at the Enfield plant. This has reduced their energy consumption by 27 per cent since 2008. Also, they were one of the first production sites in the UK to implement water efficiency systems on their running conveyor systems. This constant monitoring and updating of the manufacturing processes has meant the company can claim that no waste has been sent to landfill since 2008. These regular plant efficiency updates have allowed the production of drink to increase to 142,000 litres per hour which equates to a staggering output of 50 million cases per year.

While investing in technology does not come cheap, it is generally accepted, that in the long-term, the benefits to the company, and also to our planet's environment, outweigh the cost of the outlay. Perhaps if British manufacturers had modernised and updated their factories after the Second World War this country would not be so reliant on goods imported from abroad. Perhaps others can learn from this example!

References

Frederick, Allen, *Secret Formula: How Brilliant Marketing and Relentless Salesmanship Made Coca-Cola the Best-Known Product in the World*, New York: Harper Business (1994)

Gardiner, Richard, 'The Civil War Origin of Coca-Cola in Columbus, Georgia', *Muscogiana: Journal of the Muscogee Genealogical Society, Vol. 23* (Spring 2012)

CONCLUSION

As the reader will probably appreciate the author has not been able to include every brewery, microbrewery, food wholesaler and manufacturer within the Lea Valley region. This is due to publishing deadlines and personal time constraints. Hopefully, these omissions might encourage like-minded writers to take up the baton of research and run with it into the future. However, it is hoped that by recording some of the food and drink stories, and also the interesting backstories that this work has uncovered, we have all, including the author, learned a little more about the amazing Lea Valley region, a place that all the major historians and broadcasters continually appear to overlook.